Simple Sermons on Grace and Glory

Simple Sermons on Grace and Glory

W. Herschel Ford

BAKER BOOK HOUSE
Grand Rapids, Michigan 49506

Copyright 1977 by The Zondervan Corporation
Grand Rapids, Michigan

Reprinted 1986 by Baker Book House
Grand Rapids, Michigan
with the permission of the copyright holder

Library of Congress Catalog Card Number: 77-24412
ISBN: 0-8010-3526-0

Second printing, December 1986

Printed in the United States of America

*This book is lovingly dedicated to
my sweet great-granddaughters,
Libby and Aimee,
with all of my love.*

CONTENTS

Preface

1. The Hope of the World (Luke 4:14-22a) 13
2. The First Words of Jesus (Mark 1:21,22; John 7:45,46) 21
3. The Last Words of Jesus (Mark 1:21,22; John 7:45,46) 29
4. The Man We Want to See (John 12:21) 37
5. The University of Hard Knocks (2 Corinthians 12:7-9) 43
6. Meeting Our Sins Again (Genesis 42:21) 51
7. Behold the Man (John 19:1-6) 59
8. Precious in the Sight of the Lord (Psalm 116:15) 67
9. The Lure of the Upward Look (Psalm 121) 75
10. Christ May Return at Any Moment (Hebrews 10:37) 83

PREFACE

Two great words in the Christian vocabulary are *grace* and *glory*. Grace comes in when we are saved and operates through all of life.

> Thru many dangers, toils and snares,
>   I have already come;
> 'Tis grace hath brought me safe thus far,
>   And grace will lead me home.

Then there is glory at the end of the way when we see Jesus:

> When we've been there ten thousand years,
>   Bright shining as the sun,
> We've no less days to sing God's praise
>   Than when we'd first begun.

May this book of Christian messages lead many souls to know the saving grace that comes in this life, and may we all meet one day in glory at His blessed feet. These are your sermons now. Use anything in this book freely for Him.

W. HERSCHEL FORD

Simple Sermons on Grace and Glory

1

THE HOPE OF THE WORLD

Luke 4:14-22a

I like to hear great gospel preachers, men called of God to deliver His message. It has been my privilege to hear some of them, but there are others I wish I could have heard. I think of Spurgeon, the matchless preacher of England, who held great congregations spellbound as he talked of Jesus. I think of Dwight L. Moody, the uneducated American who "murdered" the king's English, but who also melted countless hearts for Christ. I think of Talmadge, the powerful orator whose eloquence always centered in Christ.

I wish I could have heard these men in their prime, but it would have been even more wonderful to hear the Lord Jesus, who spoke "as never man spake" before. On the Sabbath day we see Him in the synagogue. He mounts the pulpit and every eye is on Him. People nudge each other and whisper, "Isn't that Joseph's son? What is He going to do? What is He going to say?" He looks into the faces of His congregation; He sees all the sorrow and despair written there. He thinks of His mission and begins to speak. Listen to Him as He says, "The Spirit of the Lord is upon me, because he hath anointed me to preach the gospel to the poor; he hath sent me to heal the brokenhearted, to preach deliverance to the captives, and the recovering of sight to the blind, to set at liberty them that are bruised, to preach the acceptable year of the Lord."

Today we are living in a tired and sinful world. It was just as sinful in Jesus' day. Yet standing in that pulpit in Nazareth that day was the hope of the world.

Some time ago 1,200 men were gathered together in a

meeting, and a preacher said to them, "I want you to be very frank with me. Give me all the objections you have to Christianity." One man said, "Church members live inconsistent lives; they don't live up to their professions." Another said, "Preachers are not what they ought to be; they are not true to their calling." A third said, "There are too many hypocrites in the church." In all, twenty-seven objections were given. Then the preacher said, "Fellows, everything you've said is true; but I noticed one thing. Not one of you could say a word against Jesus Christ."

There is nothing wrong with Him. We must say with Pilate, "I find no fault in Him." Everything about Him is simply marvelous. He is wonderful in His birth, His life, His miracles, His sermons, His death and resurrection, His ascension, and His coming again.

Suppose Jesus had never come; suppose the angels had never sung on the Judean hills; suppose there had been no star over Bethlehem, no Sermon on the Mount, no Transfiguration, no Calvary, no resurrection morning, and no ascension. Where would this world be? It would be sunk in darkness and helplessness.

It was a great event when Adam was created, when Moses led the children of Israel out of Egypt, when David wrote the Twenty-third Psalm. But the greatest event witnessed by man and directed by God was the coming of Jesus into the world. Now, let's see what His coming meant to humanity.

I. Jesus Came to Give Hope to the Hopeless

When Christ came into the world He found man living in the unhappiest conditions humanity had ever faced. Most people were subject to a favored few. A small number were rich, but many were poor and trodden underfoot. A child was worth nothing. Herod in his time killed all those under two years of age. Neither were women worth anything; they were little more than slaves. Did these human conditions touch Jesus? Yes, in His first public sermon He said, "I have come to help you. My heart is breaking for you, but I bring you a message of hope."

The Hope of the World

A few months passed and John the Baptist was in prison, downhearted and discouraged. He sent a messenger to Jesus. "Are you the Christ, the Messiah?" he asked. "Or do we look for another?" Jesus sent back a message, "Go and tell John that the blind can see, the lame can walk, the lepers are cleansed, the dead are raised up, and the poor have the gospel preached to them." Jesus' words and deeds showed that the needs of mankind were close to His heart.

The poor were devoted to Him. "The common people heard him gladly" (Mark 12:37). They saw Him as their best friend. As He looked upon their needs, He said, "Be not overanxious; God knows, and He cares." How about the rich people? He loved them, too. He was no respecter of persons. Nicodemus was His friend; Joseph lent Him his new tomb; John used his influence at His trial; Matthew gave a feast in His honor.

Jesus was interested in everyone, the rich and the poor, the good and the bad. Everyone was important to Him. Today there are few slaves in the world; children are loved and cared for; women have a high position; and hospitals and homes are available for children and the aged. All of this because Jesus placed a high value on people.

James Martineau said, "Jesus Christ must be called the regenerator of the human race. The world has changed and Jesus is the One who changed it."

But always remember this. Although Jesus was interested in the body, His chief interest was the soul. He was interested in the earthly life, but He was even more interested in the heavenly existence. He was concerned with the ills of the flesh, but He was more concerned with the sins of the soul. He knew that the body lasts only a few years, but the soul lives on forever. That was why He wanted to see men saved. All in all, He brought hope to the hopeless.

II. Jesus Came to Give Hope to the Lost

How can a man marred by sin get into a right relationship with God? He has only to come to Christ. A poor sinner comes to Jesus and cries out, "I am a sinner. How can I find my way to God? How can I be saved?" Jesus says, "Come unto Me and I'll save you. There is no other way. I am the Way; no man cometh unto the Father except through Me."

> I must needs go home by the way of the cross,
>   There's no other way but this;
> I shall ne'er get sight of the Gates of Light,
>   If the way of the cross I miss.

When the great Temple of Karnak came tumbling down, just one flaw was found in the stone — the flaw that caused it to fall. Your life may be beautiful and wonderful, but the flaw of sin is there and will cause your eternal downfall. You need to come to Christ, who alone can erase your sin and transform your life.

Years ago on Lincoln's birthday a cartoon appeared in one of our newspapers. A log cabin was shown at the bottom of a ladder, and the White House was at the top. The caption under the cartoon read, "The ladder is still there." Earth is down here; heaven is up yonder. Jesus is the ladder anyone can climb and find God and heaven.

Dr. Samuel Chadwick of London announced a service "for infidels only." A large number of them came. They did not sing or bow their heads; they simply heckled the preacher. At the end of his sermon Dr. Chadwick invited those who wanted to discuss religion further to meet him in the vestry. Nineteen people stayed, and he said to them, "Suppose we grant that your philosophy is sufficient for a man of moral character, social position, and economic security. What would you do with those who do not have these things and whose lives have been wrecked with sin?" And the spokesman for the group answered, "Sir, we would bring them to you, for you have their only hope."

Yes, Jesus Christ is the only hope for those who have sinned. That means He is the only hope for all men; for all men have sinned, be they rich or poor, humble or great, learned or ignorant.

Do you remember the day when you gave your heart to Christ? I do. I was sixteen years old and was living in Atlanta when Billy Sunday came to that city for one of his great meetings. Many people attended out of curiosity; but when they came, they saw God's power at work. On Sunday afternoon I went to hear him for the third or fourth time. He preached his sermon, then jumped down from the pulpit and urged sinners to come forward and receive Christ. Moved by the Holy Spirit, I walked down the aisle and put my hand in Billy Sunday's hand. But I did more than that; I placed my hand in the nail-pierced hand of Jesus Christ. I looked beyond the great evangelist and saw my Savior dying for me. That day I gave Him my heart and soul.

> I saw One hanging on a tree
> In agony and blood,
> He fixed His languid eyes on me,
> As near His cross I stood.
>
> Sure, never till my latest breath,
> Can I forget that look;
> It seemed to charge me with His death,
> Though not a word He spoke.
>
> My conscience felt and owned the guilt,
> And plunged me in despair;
> I saw my sins His blood had spilt
> And helped to nail Him there.
>
> Alas, I know not what I did,
> But now my tears are vain;
> Where can my trembling soul be hid?
> For I the Lord have slain.
>
> A second look He gave, which said,
> "I freely all forgive;
> This blood is for thy ransom paid,
> I die that thou may'st live!"
>
> Oh, can it be, upon that tree,
> The Savior died for me?
> My soul is filled, my heart is thrilled
> To think He died for me.

Lost man, there is no hope except in Jesus Christ.

III. JESUS CAME TO TELL US WHAT KIND OF GOD WE HAVE

How does God feel about us? Does He love us? Does He care when life hurts us? What kind of being is He? And Jesus answers, "He that hath seen Me hath seen the Father. As you see Me loving, lifting, blessing, you know the kind of God He is. He cares for the lilies of the field; He sees the sparrow as it falls; and He cares for you."

There is a king sitting in council. His little girl falls nearby and begins to weep. The king leaves the council table and rushes over to pick her up, soothe her, and wipe away her tears. This action elevates the king in our estimation. Well, God is upon His throne. He is busy with the whole universe and its people. But when we fall and cry out to Him, He rushes to help us. Thus we know the kind of God He is.

Two missionaries walked through a heathen temple in India. They saw a woman with a sick child in her arms. She lifted the child up toward heaven and prayed. "To whom are you praying?" one of the missionaries asked. And the woman said, "I don't know, but there ought to be someone somewhere who will hear a mother's prayer and keep her heart from breaking." O mother of the broken heart, there *is* Someone. O soul bowed down in grief, there *is* Someone. O friend burdened with sin, there *is* Someone. Jesus came to tell us that God is a loving Father.

So come with your sorrows and burdens. Look up into His face and say, "O Thou who didst sweat drops of blood in Gethsemane's garden, Thou who didst suffer and die on Calvary's tree, remember me." And He will do just that. He will reach down His loving arms, put them around you, and give you peace.

IV. Jesus Came to Tell Us How to Make Our Lives Worthwhile

We want to know how to be useful and how to find happiness. Where do we get the answer? From Christ, who said, "Happiness does not consist in the things you possess; he that would find his life must lose it."

Napoleon said, "I will get power and then I'll be happy." He brought Europe to its knees; he made thousands of widows and orphans; he gained world-wide fame. But he died an exile, a broken man. The world would not say that his life counted.

During the Civil War a man was picked up on the battlefield, fearfully wounded. He promised God that if He would heal him, he would give the Lord the rest of his life. The years went by and eventually the man died. What had he done? He had built a great church; he had built two hospitals and a great university; he had sent thousands of young people to school. Russell Conwell's life counted, for it was centered in Christ.

Once upon a time there was an Oriental king. Each day he dressed himself in his resplendent uniform, put on his medals, and strutted up and down before his mirror. He thought only of himself, while his people suffered and starved. But one of his elder statesmen realized there was some good in the man if he could get his mind off himself and think of his people. So one night the statesman tore out the mirror and placed a window where it had been. The next morning the king came down to admire himself in the mirror. Instead he looked out the window and saw his people. He saw a weary mother and her children; he saw tired men bent low under heavy burdens; he saw hungry children scrounging for food in garbage cans. He even saw a beautiful young woman. Abruptly he removed his uniform, dressed in simple clothes, and went out among his people. He learned their needs and set about to relieve their suffering. He even found a beautiful wife for himself.

Yes, Jesus would say, "If you want to find happiness, look away from yourself. Give your life away to the service of God and man."

V. Jesus Came to Give Us Hope About the Future Life

Long ago a man asked the question, "If a man die shall he live again?" Jesus answered that question. "Yes," He said, "if a man believes in Me he shall live forever. Just trust Me, and I'll take care of you out there."

Before He came there was no light beyond the grave; it was all darkness and mystery. For thousands of years men had marched in an unbroken column toward the shadows. And of all the millions who went down into the grave, none came back. There was no voice from beyond. But Jesus came and said, "There is a back door to the grave. It opens up into heaven for all who believe. Fear not; I am the Resurrection and the Life. If a man believe in Me, even though he dies, yet shall he live again."

The Bible says, "Blessed are the dead who die in the Lord, . . . for they rest from their labors; and their works do follow them. . . . Absent from the body, . . . present with the Lord. . . . So shall we ever be with the Lord. . . . I go to prepare a place for you. . . . For me to live is Christ, and to die is gain."

When General MacArthur left Bataan, he said, "I shall return." His soldiers were imprisoned by the Japanese. Months went by and they suffered many things. One day the American tanks rolled up to the gates of the prison. "Open up," the command rang out; but the Japanese refused. The American soldiers set their tanks at "full power ahead" and crashed the gates. All the prisoners began to shout and rejoice. One man in the back of the camp was too weak to come out. He wondered at the noise and commotion. A buddy went in, told him what had happened, and carried him back to the center of the camp. That prisoner bowed down and thanked God, crying out, "Free, free at last."

Death may conquer us; graves may hold our bodies for a while. But Jesus is coming back; our bodies will be raised and made like His own glorious body; and we shall be free — free to go up and live with Him forever and ever. Thank God!

Yes, Jesus is our hope in all things — our hope in life and death and in the great beyond. Oh, how we ought to love Him!

2

THE FIRST WORDS OF JESUS

Mark 1:21,22; John 7:45,46

What a man says reveals what he is. Jesus said, "Out of the abundance of the heart the mouth speaketh" (Matt. 12:34). Did you ever think of the power of words? Hitler whipped Germany into a frenzy of hate by his words and thus brought on World War II. Franklin D. Roosevelt roused America to a high pitch of patriotic emotion by his "fireside chats." Spurgeon, Wesley, Whitefield, Moody, Finney, and Sunday led thousands into the kingdom by the use of words.

But, oh, the words of Jesus — how powerful they must have been! They have come thundering down the ages to convict and convince, to condemn and convert. One day He went into the synagogue and taught great things about God and men. The people listened intently to Him and went out shaking their heads, saying, "He taught as one having authority and not as the scribes."

On one occasion the chief priests and Pharisees sent officers to arrest Him, and they came back empty-handed, saying, "We could not arrest Him. No man ever spoke as this man speaks." And men of all the ages have marveled at the words of Jesus. In this chapter I speak to you of the first words of Jesus. In the next chapter I will speak of the last words of Jesus.

I. "KNOW YE NOT THAT I MUST BE ABOUT MY FATHER'S BUSINESS?" (LUKE 2:49)

You will remember the story. When Jesus was twelve years of age, Joseph and Mary took Him to Jerusalem to attend the Feast of the Passover. They spent several days there having fellowship with their friends and loved ones and going through the forms of their ceremonial religion. When they were ready to leave, I can imagine that Mary said to Joseph, "Where is Jesus?" And Joseph replied, "I think He is with Jacob. I saw them together last night." Then they went to Jacob's group, but they hadn't seen Him.

Mary and Joseph were terrified and rushed back to the city. They didn't look for Him at some show or game; they went to God's house and found Him there having a discussion with the teachers about the great things of God. They rebuked Him and said, "Why have You done this? We have sought You sorrowing." And He answered, "Don't you know that I must be about My Father's business?"

All through life He kept the same spirit. He said, "I must work the works of him that sent me . . . the night cometh when no man can work" (John 9:4). And He kept on working until on the cross He could say, "It is finished." Today His business is still the greatest on earth. It is a far greater business than that of General Motors or Standard Oil. There is no business as great as God's business.

For us who belong to Christ there is but one task, that of carrying on God's business wherever we are, winning others to Him. Dr. George W. Truett said, "If I had a thousand lives, I would give every one of them to God as a gospel preacher." And Phillips Brooks said, "I feel sorry for all of you who are not parsons."

They were simply saying that God's business is our business and that it is the greatest business on earth. But His business is not confined to preachers. It should be the chief concern of every Christian. What business are we in? The work of His church and the winning of lost souls.

Today we hear much about "the new evangelism." But it is social, not redemptive. A prominent preacher recently said, "The church needs to be concerned with pressing human needs, such as world hunger, prison reform, and distribution of decision-making powers." The big word is *involvement* — let's get involved in all the movements around us; let's join the picket line; let's demonstrate. Another common word is

The First Words of Jesus

dialogue — let's lay aside the Bible, get together, and discuss our differences in human terms. Another saying is, "Let's make the gospel relevant." But it has always been relevant; it fits the need of every man.

In the "new evangelism" there is nothing about sin or salvation, judgment, heaven, or hell. There is no word for the lost man, no strength to live by, no grace to die by.

Today people say, "We must get out where the action is." But we don't hear of anyone being saved out there by humanistic involvement. Our primary task is to win people to Christ, yet this work is almost a lost art. We are not to depend on our intelligence, our pulpit eloquence, our striving for numbers, or our church programs, but simply upon the power of the Holy Spirit working through us.

One of our large denominations had a conference some time ago. The newspapers reported that they discussed communism, the race question, ecumenism, and artificial insemination. But there was not one word for the souls of lost men. Many groups are speaking about abortion, birth control, war, and peace, but nothing about the New Birth, without which there is no hope for anyone. Jesus said, "I must be about My Father's business." That's where you and I ought to be also.

II. "Suffer It to Be So Now: For Thus it Becometh Us to Fulfil All Righteousness"

John the Baptist was a great country preacher. He did not have to go to the city to draw a crowd. The people came out in great numbers and stood on the banks of the river to hear him preach. One day Jesus came and said to John, "I want you to baptize Me." "Oh, no," replied John. "I should be baptized by You, not You by me." "Suffer it to be so now," said Jesus, "for in this way we will fulfill all righteousness."

So Jesus went down into the water and John baptized Him. When He came up out of the water, with His clothes dripping wet, the Holy Spirit in the form of a dove descended on Him; and a voice from heaven, God's voice, said, "This is my beloved Son, in whom I am well pleased" (Matt. 3:17).

Christ's baptism furnishes the pattern for every redeemed

soul. What is the first desire of every convert? It is: "Now I want to follow Christ in baptism. I want to be obedient to His holy command." You may never preach a sermon, but in baptism you are preaching about the death, burial, and resurrection of Christ — death and burial of the old life, and resurrection to a newness of life. You also preach a prophetic sermon, showing forth the fact that when He comes again, we shall all be raised in the Resurrection.

Baptism has no saving grace about it. It is simply a matter of obedience. You can be saved without baptism, but you can't be an obedient child of God without it. And the Christian's life should be one of obedience. Jesus said, "I do always those things that please him" (John 8:29). And Paul said, "I was not disobedient unto the heavenly vision" (Acts 26:19).

I know that peace and happiness can be found in the will of God and not in any other way of life. A young lady said to Dr. L. R. Scarborough, "I do not need your Christ, I am all right as I am." Led by the Spirit of God, Dr. Scarborough said to her, "Young lady, is God calling you to some special service?" She broke down and confessed that God had called her to be a missionary. She had turned down His call, and her life had become miserable. No Christian finds happiness until he finds it in the will of God.

III. "Repent Ye, and Believe the Gospel" (Mark 1:15)

After His baptism and temptation, Jesus went into Galilee, preaching that the kingdom of God was at hand and calling on men to repent.

The question many are asking today is, "How can I get through to God?" We get to Him simply by coming to Christ, who said, "No man cometh to the Father except through me." And He is anxiously waiting for us to repent and come to Him in faith. He lives for that purpose. He is not a distant God; He "is nearer than hands and feet and closer than breathing." He is so big He covers the world; He is so small He can live in our hearts.

Those who want Him can find Him when they seek him with their whole heart. People seek Him in different ways. The savage seeks Him by cutting and mutilating himself. The pagan seeks Him by bowing down before some image or statue. In Japan I saw a great statue of Buddha, with gifts spread out before him and people worshiping him. Civilized men seek Him through religious forms and customs.

But all through the Old Testament, men were called on to repent. In the New Testament John the Baptist, Jesus, Peter, and Paul preached repentance. And every great preacher since those days has had this as his central theme.

Repentance is a biblical doctrine, but it is not pleasant to the natural man, because it involves turning from his sin. Repentance is not merely the fear of God. Many men, afraid they are near death, cry out to God in fear, but that is not repentance. It is not simply sorrow for sin or conviction about sin or an empty confession of sin. Repentance goes deeper than that and changes the whole life.

Repentance is a complete change of heart and life. It involves turning from sin to the Savior, coming over on God's side and taking His side against our sin.

It is a continuous change. Sins come into our lives every day, and every day we should be repenting of those sins and turning back to God. He who is born of God does not continue in his old sin; he does not "practice" sin any more.

"And the times of this ignorance God overlooked, but now commandeth all men everywhere to repent" (Acts 17:30 RSV). This is the first step to God and should always be preached.

IV. "WHAT SEEK YE?" (JOHN 1:38)

One day John was talking to two of his disciples. He saw Jesus approaching and said, "Behold the Lamb of God." Then these two disciples of John left him and followed Jesus. What a beautiful picture we see here. The true preacher does not point to himself but to Jesus. This caused these men to follow the Savior. Jesus turned and said to them, "What seek ye?" and they replied, "Master, where dwellest thou?" And Jesus said, "Come and see." They went with Him, spent the day in His presence, and I am sure they heard some of the greatest teachings they had ever heard.

One of these men was Andrew, Simon Peter's brother. Andrew immediately went after Peter and did the greatest thing he could do for his brother: "And he brought him to Jesus." A chain of soul-winning began which was climaxed at Pentecost when 3000 were saved.

"What seek ye?" What are men seeking today? Pleasure, profit, peace, and power. They go to the extremes to find these things because they are looking for them in the wrong places. Christ Himself is still the answer to man's needs.

Mr. H. G. Spafford was a businessman in Chicago. He had a beautiful home, a lovely wife, and two precious children. In the great Chicago fire his home burned. His family stood on a hill and wept as they watched it go up in flames. Mr. Spafford borrowed some money and sent his wife and children to Europe to stay with some friends until he could get on his feet again. In the middle of the Atlantic the ship went down. Mrs. Spafford held her children in her arms until a heavy wave swept them out of her arms and into the sea. She was rescued and sent her husband a sad telegram, "Saved alone." Mr. Spafford went down into the valley of the shadow, but out of his experience he wrote the song:

> When peace, like a river, attendeth my way,
> When sorrows like sea-billows roll;
> Whatever my lot, Thou hast taught me to say,
> It is well, it is well with my soul.

Where can a person find that which permanently satisfies? Not in science, in profit, in worldly pleasures, or in earthly honors. One can find satisfaction only in Christ. A dear woman in Atlanta said to me when her daughter died, "What would I do now without Jesus?" And what would we do in the dark hours if we did not have Him?

So as we listen to the words of Jesus, we find wisdom for our years, guidance for our lives, strength for our needs, comfort for our sorrows, and a home for our souls.

General John B. Gordon was running for the position of United States senator from Georgia. One group of men bitterly opposed him and selected a man to go up to Atlanta and vote against him in the legislature. Those were the days when senators were elected by the legislature rather than by popular vote. When election day came, General Gordon was elected. The man who was instructed to vote against him voted for him instead and helped to elect him.

General Gordon's political enemies called a meeting and brought before them the man who had promised to vote against Gordon, but who had voted for him instead. "Why did you break your promise to us?" they asked. "We sent you up to Atlanta to vote against Gordon. Instead you voted for him and assured his election. Why did you betray us?"

"Gentlemen," the man answered, "I had never seen General Gordon. One day as I stood in the legislative halls talking to another man, I saw a striking man come in. I noticed that he had a livid scar running down one side of his face. I asked my friend who this man was and he said, 'Why, don't you know him? That's General Gordon who is running for a place in the United States Senate.' And, gentlemen, when I looked upon that scarred face and realized that he had fought my battles and had been wounded in my behalf, I could not find it in my heart to vote against him."

When we realize what the Lord Jesus Christ has done for us. how can we find it in our hearts to be less than 100 percent faithful to Him? Let us be faithful by giving Him our very best every day; and when we meet Him and hear Him say, "Well done," that will be the sweetest music our ears have ever heard.

3

THE LAST WORDS OF JESUS

Mark 1:21,22; John 7:45,46

The last words of a man, just before he goes out into eternity, often hold special significance.

Just before Tom Paine, the prominent infidel and author, went out to meet his Maker, he said, "I would give worlds if I hadn't written 'The Age of Reason.' Oh, Lord, help me. Oh, Christ, help me. Stay with me, for God's sake. Send even a little child to stay with me, for it is hell to be alone. If the devil ever had an agent, I am that one." Men ought not to die like that, but Paine died as he had lived.

The great missionary Adoniram Judson said, "I go with the gladness of a boy bounding away from school, I am so strong in Christ."

Catherine Booth, the Salvation Army worker, said, "The waters are rising but so am I. I am not going under, but over. Do not be concerned about dying; go on living for Christ and dying will be all right."

Stonewall Jackson said, "I am just going across the river and rest beneath the shade of the trees on the other side."

But the last words of Jesus came not when He was dying, but after He had died and risen again. The Resurrection sets Him apart from all other men. He is the only One who conquered death and came back to tell us about it.

I. IN MATTHEW, MARK, AND ACTS WE FIND SOME PART OF THE GREAT COMMISSION

All three references are summed up in the words, "Go ye into all the world, win men to Christ, baptize them, and teach them all that I have commanded thee, and I'll be with you all the way." That's the reason we are in the biggest business in the world.

A man said to a preacher, "What does the church have to offer that is offered nowhere else in the world?" The answer came quickly, "The church offers Jesus Christ. He is not offered anywhere else." This is the purpose of the church: to present Jesus Christ to the world. Today many are getting away from God's program. They don't believe the Word; consequently, they are not trying to carry out the Great Commission.

One year the National Council of Churches met for their annual meeting in Miami. Their leaders came together, men and women, preachers and laymen who are supposed to follow Christ. A poll was taken and these were the results:

> 33 percent were not sure that God existed
> 36 percent did not believe that Jesus Christ was the divine Son of God
> 31 percent did not believe in a life after death
> 62 percent did not believe that the miracles happened.

The time was spent in dialogue, discussing ecumenicism, politics, and the social welfare programs of America. But that is not God's program as given in His Book. He calls men to go out and tell about Him. What will these other things mean when men are dying in sin and going to hell?

What happens when men stop proclaiming the full gospel of Christ? The world goes wrong. We have seen it in our country. We see riots and rapes, graft, disregard for law, sin on every side. I believe the majority of this has come about because God and His gospel have been forsaken.

The National Conferences of Churches was holding some meetings on the campus of Notre Dame. Let me quote something that happened there.

> Something of a bombshell was dropped by Dr. Ernest van den Haag, professor of Social Philosophy at New York University and at the new school of graduate studies in New York City. Called in to present an "outsider's" viewpoint, he amazed all the delegates and delighted many conservatives by challenging Christian ministers to "stick by their business" of preaching the

gospel of salvation from sin instead of dissipating their energies at tasks in which they have no business and, as often as not, no special abilities. By turning to social, political, and other issues, the church and the Christian ministry today have lost their relevance. 'Get back to the church's real business of personal faith," was the psychoanalyst's plea.

In the maze of terminology one word has been lost — the word *compassion,* compassion for lost sinners. Jeremiah cried out, "Is it nothing to you?" And David lamented, "No man cared for my soul." We have many organizations set up in our churches, but how much do we care for the souls of men? In one of my churches we gave a banquet for those who had finished all the study-course books on Christian activities. At the head table sat a man who had taken every course. But when someone approached him about going out to seek the conversion of a teen-age boy, he declined, saying, "I don't know how to do anything like that." He had missed the whole meaning of the studies.

One Christmas Eve Dr. Robert G. Lee sat by the fireside with his wife when the telephone rang. "I wish you didn't have to answer it," she said, "you have so few evenings at home." But he did answer the phone and a nurse from the hospital said, "Dr. Lee, can you come over to the hospital? A young woman has attempted suicide, and we're afraid she won't last long." Dr. Lee went to the young woman's room in the hospital. He tried to get the message of salvation over to her, but she was too far gone to understand him. She died as Dr. Lee stood by the bedside. He went home and his wife met him at the door and said to him, "What's the matter, honey? Are you sick?" "No," he answered, "but I stood by a bedside tonight and watched a young woman die and go to hell."

As we read the Gospels, we see that the last three times Jesus spoke before He went away He was saying, "There are many lost people in the world; do everything you can to win them."

II. "Tarry Ye . . . Until Ye Be Endued With Power From on High" (Luke 24:49)

Look at Christ's disciples. They had had an experience they

would never get over, a thrill that shook their souls. They had seen a man die and come back to life again. Now they wanted to rush out and tell the whole world about it. "Let's go!" they cried. But Jesus said, "Wait. You are not ready yet. Wait until you are endued with power from on high." They waited and prayed for ten days, the power fell upon them, and they went out to turn the world upside down for Christ.

Isn't this our trouble? We go to school and get our degrees, we study all the modern methods, we have our meetings, we preach and sing, and nothing happens. We need more than human resources to do God's work; we need the supernatural power of the Holy Spirit.

There are two primary functions of the Holy Spirit in a believer's life. First, there is the baptism of the Holy Spirit, which comes the minute one is saved. Jesus said that the Holy Spirit would abide with us forever. When we are saved, the Holy Spirit comes to live in our hearts. Sometimes we push Him into a tiny corner, but He is still there. Then He comes to infill us for service as we have need of Him and meet His conditions.

Before there can be a filling, there must be an emptying. Sin, self, worldliness, and indifference must be thrown out. Any cloud between us and Him must be removed.

Ephesians 5:18 says, "Be not drunk with wine, wherein is excess; but be filled with the Spirit." The last part of this verse applies to all Christians, as does the first part. There is an analogy here. Often the shy man can talk without inhibition when he gets drunk; he can sing although he has never sung a note; he thinks he is strong enough to whip anyone in the house. In like manner a person is an altogether different human being when he is filled with the Holy Spirit. He is altogether changed.

III. "FOLLOW THOU ME" (JOHN 21:22)

Peter was curious about what would happen to John in later years. So He turned to Jesus and asked, "What shall this man do?" And Jesus, in effect, said, "That's none of your business, Peter, follow thou Me." He is still saying that today.

We are to follow Him in full surrender. A. T. Pierson said to George Muller, "What is the secret of your rich life and great success?" And Muller humbly answered, "There was a time when I died to George Muller." Yes, it is the life that dies to the world and self that counts.

It costs a full surrender of life to serve Him. When God called me to preach, it was so definite I felt I would die if I did not obey Him. I didn't even have a high school education. I had quit school earlier in my life. When I made it known to the other members of my family, they hooted at the idea. Every time I brought up the matter they would ridicule me. I had opposition on every side. But I kept on saying, "God has called me to preach and I must not turn a deaf ear to His call. I know I am not at all qualified, but I am trusting Him to help me." In the course of time, even though I was already married and had two children, He made it possible for me to go to school and prepare for an active ministry of more than fifty years.

Often, when some young man tells me that God has called Him to preach but he is not prepared for it, I tell him my story and say, "If God could do that for me, with all the handicaps and opposition, I am sure He can do it for you, if you make a full surrender to Him and His will." God never fails one who can say from his heart, "All to Jesus I surrender."

The surrendered person is always to lead a warm devotional life. It is so easy for one to get far away from God, to follow Him only at a distance. Dr. Carter Helm Jones told about a time when he was extremely busy with many activities. But on the top floor of his house he had a secluded room where he went when he got away with God in his devotional life. One day he told his wife that he was going up to that room for a few minutes. He had been there only a short time when he heard a patter of steps on the stairs and a timid knock at the door. When he opened the door, his little girl was standing outside, and he said to her in a gruff manner, "Now what do you want?" "Nothing, daddy," she replied. "You've been so busy lately I haven't gotten to love you any. I just wanted to love you a little." He dropped to his knees and hugged and kissed her, and then his little daughter scampered back down the stairs.

Then the preacher got on his knees by the chair and said, "Lord, that's what I need. I've been so busy lately at other things that I haven't had time to love You. Now I do want to love You awhile." And when he went back downstairs, he felt much better.

We are the channels through which the gospel must flow. Those channels are always to be clean and open. That gospel must come down to the world from God through clean and chosen vessels. One great preacher said, "I shudder to think of what would have happened and what my life would have been if I had not made a full surrender to Him."

IV. "Surely I Come Quickly" (Revelation 22:20)

1. *What is the greatest thing that could happen to the world?* Not world-wide peace, although that would be great. Not decent housing and clothing and food for the world. Not a cure for cancer and heart trouble. Not the winning of the space race. Not ridding the world of prejudice and communism. No, the greatest thing that could happen to the world would be the return of the Lord, for He would straighten out all these other matters and give us peace, plenty, prosperity, and joy abounding.

2. *What will happen when He comes?*

> But I would not have you to be ignorant, brethren, concerning them which are asleep, that ye sorrow not, even as others which have no hope. For if we believe that Jesus died and rose again, even so them also which sleep in Jesus will God bring with him. For this we say unto you by the word of the Lord, that we which are alive and remain unto the coming of the Lord shall not prevent (precede) them which are asleep. For the Lord himself shall descend from heaven with a shout, with the voice of the archangel, and with the trump of God: and the dead in Christ shall rise first: then we which are alive and remain shall be caught up together with them in the clouds, to meet the Lord in the air: and so shall we ever be with the Lord. Wherefore comfort one another with these words (1 Thess. 4:13-18).

Christ will come in the air. The dead in Christ will be raised; their spirits and bodies will be joined together; and their salvation will be complete. The Christians still living will be caught up to meet the others in the air. Tribulation will take place on the earth, but God's people will be in heaven with Christ. Jesus will then come back to earth with His people and the thousand-year period will begin. At the end of that time the lost will be raised and the eternal ages will begin, with the saved in heaven and the lost in hell.

3. *What will Christ find when He comes?* He will find some people greatly surprised. He will find scoffers on every hand. He will find a great falling away, and we certainly see that today. All opportunities to be saved will be over. All opportunities to serve Him will be over.

When is He coming back? No one knows. Even Jesus Himself said He didn't know. But when we look at the world conditions today, when we see His prophecies being fulfilled on every side, we believe that His coming must be near. When the last one who is to be saved has been saved, He will come. I want Him to find me faithful when He comes.

What is Jesus saying in His last important words? "Get busy for Me, telling others about Me, winning them to Me. Follow close to Me, and I'll give you power to serve Me. Then when I come I'll bring you a reward."

One of our preachers was conducting a revival in one of our churches. Only one black person attended, and she sat alone in the balcony. One morning the pastor gave the people an opportunity to stand and give a testimony of what the Lord had done for them. This dear black woman stood and said, "You all know me and my daughter, Lilly. Some time ago I found Lilly crying, and she told me the Lord had called her to be a missionary. She said she wanted to go and serve Him, but she did not have the education that was needed and didn't have the money to go to school. Then I said to her, 'Don't worry about that, Lilly. I'll work hard and save the money so you can go to school.'" That mother worked hard and sent Lilly to school. In due time Lilly graduated and the Foreign Mission Board sent her to Africa as a missionary.

In telling her story the dear soul said, "You people know how hard I worked and saved to send Lilly to school; now she's over there winning souls to Jesus in Africa. Someday Jesus is going to give Lilly a crown for her work; but you know, I believe He's going to have a crown for me, too."

Yes, He'll have a crown and reward for all who serve Him. God help us to be faithful and win that crown.

4

THE MAN WE WANT TO SEE

John 12:21

If we had been in Jerusalem on a certain day, we would have seen a great crowd making its way down toward the temple. If we had not known the particular significance of that day, if we had not known why all the people were there, we would have said to some passer-by, "Why are all the people gathered here, and what is going on down at the temple?" And he would have answered, "Why, didn't you know this is the day of the Passover Feast, and our people have gathered from far and near to observe this solemn and important occasion?"

Then we would have remembered. Our minds would go back into Jewish history and we would remember this occasion. It was a day the Jews never forgot. The people of God were in bondage in Egypt. They were slaves under cruel taskmasters; their lot in life was a hard one. But they cried out to God, and God heard them.

He sent His servant Moses to deliver them. After many strange occurrences under the eye of God, the fatal night in Egypt arrived. God said to His people, "You are to kill a lamb without spot or blemish and put his blood on the doorposts or lintels of your door. On that night My death angel will fly over you. If the blood is not there, every firstborn in the land of Egypt will die, but not even a dog will move his tongue against My people."

"And," said God, "when I see the blood, I will pass over you, and you will be safe." That night death came to the homes of the Egyptians, but God's people were spared. And God told His people that they should keep the Passover forever. This is why the Jews were in Jerusalem that day — to celebrate the Feast of the Passover.

But on that particular day there was One there who appreciated the real meaning of the Passover. Jesus was there. He knew He was the Lamb without spot or blemish. He knew He was the Lamb who would be slain. And He knew that if His blood was applied to men's souls they would be safe in Him forever. Yes, the Lord Jesus knew the true meaning of the Passover.

But there were others present also. Certain Greeks were among them who came to worship at the feast. They came not to worship, but to see the One whose fame had spread everywhere. They came to see Jesus. So they approached Philip, one of Jesus' disciples, and said to him, "Sir, we would see Jesus." So far as we can determine the Greeks did have an interview with Jesus. I know they were blessed by it, and I hope they put their trust in Him for time and eternity.

"We would see Jesus." That is the agelong cry of all humanity. "Show us the Father," they said, "and that will be sufficient." And in due time Jesus came and showed men the Father in His own Person. He said, "The Father and I are one. He that hath seen me hath seen the Father." And when men looked upon the just and loving face of Jesus, they were looking right into the heart of God. The cry of men today is just the same as it was in that faraway day, "Just show us the Father and it is sufficient." Let us look at some occasions today when we want to see Jesus.

I. WE WANT TO SEE JESUS WHEN WE ARE BURDENED WITH SIN

Read David's great confession in Psalm 51. It is the cry of a sin-sick soul trying to get back into fellowship with God. "Have mercy upon me, O God," he cries, "According to thy lovingkindness: according unto the multitude of thy tender mercies blot out my transgressions. Wash me throughly from mine iniquity, and cleanse me from my sin" (vv. 1,2). Can you imagine the man "after God's own heart" humbling himself that way before God? His was just a sin-sick soul saying, "I would see Jesus."

A young man who had gone down into the depths of sin attended the first revival I ever conducted. He was guilty of every sin in the book. But God convicted him of his sin, and he was gloriously converted. Afterwards he would often give his testimony. He said, "When I walked down that church aisle to give my heart to Jesus, it seemed that the weight of the whole world was pressing down upon me. But when I came to Christ and He saved me, the load was lifted and became as light as a feather." Why? Because he had seen Jesus, and his sins had been washed away.

We, too, carry the burden of sin. There is only one way to get rid of that burden. We must bring it to Jesus; He is our great Sin Bearer. Saved people carry sins, and lost people carry sins. Bring them all to Jesus — He will take the burden away.

II. We Want to See Jesus When We Are Engaged in Holy Worship

This was a time of religious chaos and confusion in Jerusalem. Men could come to the temple and go through all of their religious ceremonies, but the sin and guilt would still be there. There would be no peace in their hearts. A person may go to church today, go through all the forms of religious worship, and yet not truly see Jesus and have his sins washed away.

We want to see Jesus in the songs we sing. There ought to be a real Christian message in every song used in our churches. And may the Lord deliver us from those songs where we hear only the voices of the singers, but can't understand one word of the song. The really great songs, the ones that move and bless our hearts, are those written out of the deep heart experiences of men. Some years ago two men wrote a song about the scarcity of bananas, called "Yes, We Have No Bananas." How many people do you think received a blessing out of that song? Yet the writers received $25,000 from it.

We want to see Jesus in the sermons that are preached. We fail miserably in our preaching if we don't present Jesus to the people. A young preacher went to a new church as pastor. He thought the people wanted to hear intellectual preaching, witty epigrams, and high-sounding phrases, so he filled his sermons with these things. His church's attendance began to fall off. The young people left the church. Then one day when he came to his pulpit, he found a card with the words, "We would see Jesus," written on it. He was angry at first but soon began to realize he had been giving his people the wrong messages. He promised the Lord that from that time on he would preach "Christ and Him crucified." As he did this, his congregation began to grow, and the young people returned to his church. One Sunday morning when he came to his pulpit he found another card. This one said, "Then were the people glad when they saw Jesus in their midst."

III. WE WANT TO SEE JESUS IN THE DETAILS OF DAILY LIFE

A young man, who worked in a machine shop, was saved. He told me a few days later that his job seemed easier, the hours shorter, and the boss more agreeable. The circumstances were the same, but now he had Jesus for a daily Companion and Savior.

IV. WE WANT TO SEE JESUS IN OUR SORROWS AND SHADOWS

In the midnight hours we want to see the Light of the World. When the sisters in Bethany lost their brother, they immediately sent for Jesus. He's the One we want to see when sorrow comes. He's the only One who understands and can comfort us. Some people are beaten into the dust when sorrow comes; they don't know which way to turn. Others have the peace of God written upon their faces, for they have looked through their tears and have seen the Great Comforter.

One of the young ladies of our congregation died very suddenly. In those days the body was brought to the home before being taken to the church for the funeral. I went to the home, passed by the casket, the many flowers, and the friends who had gathered, and went on to say some word of comfort to the grieving mother. A young preacher with little experience, I didn't know what to say to her. But I didn't have to say anything. She put her hands in mine and said to me, "What would I do now without Jesus?" And I wonder what we would do in the dark hours without Him.

V. We Want to See Jesus in the Hour of Death

When we go down into the dark valley, we want to find Him there. And He'll be there, for He has promised to go with us through the dark valley of the shadow.

A wounded soldier kept saying, "Where is He? Where is He?" They brought in his captain, but that wasn't whom he wanted to see. Finally, when he was in a lucid moment the nurse said to him, "All day long you've been asking for someone. Whom did you want to see?" And the soldier said, "Why, don't you know, nurse? My mother taught me that Jesus would be with me when I came to the end of the way. Now, where is He?" The nurse didn't know what to say and turned away. Soon the soldier called her back to the bedside and said, "There He is, nurse. He's with me now, and I am going home with Him." And in a few minutes he was gone.

> When ends life's transient dream,
> When death's cold, sullen stream
> Shall o'er me roll,
> Blest Saviour, then, in love,
> Fear and distrust remove;
> O bear me safe above,
> A ransomed soul!

VI. We Want to See Jesus in Glory

He has promised that to us. Beyond death and the grave and this old life we want to see Him. There are many others in heaven we want to see, but most of all we want to see Jesus. We want to see Him and fall at His feet and thank Him for bringing us "home."

> Oh, the dear ones in glory,
> How they beckon me to come,
> And our parting at the river I recall;
> To the sweet vales of Eden
> They will sing my welcome home,
> But I long to meet my Saviour first of all.

Yes, we want to see Him, to feel His arms around us, to have Him wipe away all of our tears and give us perfect happiness.

Just after World War I the man who was then Prince of Wales was visiting the various rehabilitation camps. He went from bed to bed speaking to the wounded soldiers who were still there. He shook hands with those who still had hands and thanked them for their sacrifices for his country. He came out of one ward and said to the commanding officer, "How many men do you have here?" And the officer replied, "Thirty-six." "I counted only twenty-seven in there. Where are the other nine?" "They're in another room, Your Majesty," he replied, "but you cannot see them. They are so badly wounded that we don't want you to see them." "I must see them," said the prince. "They fought my battles, and they were wounded in my behalf." Well, royalty must have its way, so the prince was escorted to a room on the back side of the camp. He greeted the men who were there, thanked them for their service, shook a hand where he could find one, and came out, tears glistening in his eyes.

"I counted only eight men in there," said the prince, "where is the other man?" And the officer replied, "O prince, you would not want to see him. He has been so torn by shot and shell that he is almost unrecognizable. He stays in that one room, and the only one who sees him is the orderly who looks after him." "Yes," said the prince, "I must see him. He fought my battles — he was wounded in my behalf." Again royalty had its way, so the prince was taken to a lone room, where lay a man whose limbs had been shot away and whose face was almost gone, but who miraculously lived.

The prince did not know what to say or do. There was no hand he could grasp. Then in a moment of tense emotion he leaned over and kissed every scar that he could see on the neck and breast of the wounded soldier.

Friends, Jesus did more than that for us. We were lost and full of sin but he took us in His arms and in His death he bore all of our sins away and gave us eternal life. No wonder we want to see Him and thank Him. But we'll never see Him or have eternal life until we turn away from all of our sin and put all of our trust in Him for time and eternity. Will you do just that and do it now?

5

THE UNIVERSITY OF HARD KNOCKS

2 Corinthians 12:7-9

There are many great universities in our land. Everyone in America knows about Harvard, Yale, Princeton, and the other great schools. In England they are rightfully proud of Oxford University and its influence. In Germany there were many great schools, but they became so filled with liberalism and false ideologies that they helped to bring on two brutal world wars.

But I want to tell you about another school. It has had more students and more graduates than any other school that ever existed. Its tuition fees are the costliest on earth, but the lessons we learn there do more for us than those in any other school. I am speaking of the University of Hard Knocks.

The apostle Paul received his degree from the University of Tarsus. He sat at the feet of Gamaliel and other great teachers of that day. But he learned far more from the University of Hard Knocks, for there he sat under God's great teaching.

In the text he tells us that he had a "thorn in the flesh," which buffeted him. We don't know what it was; the Bible does not tell us. For some reason God has kept this knowledge from us. Surely that is best, for if He had revealed this knowledge, many of us would say, "That doesn't apply to me, for I have no such thorn."

As it is, the text could apply to any of us. The thorn could be any affliction, any trouble, anything that keeps us from being what we ought to be. But even though the thorns are there, God's consolations are always available to us.

Paul prayed, "O Father, remove this thorn from my flesh." Did God do that? No, God doesn't always answer our prayers exactly as we ask. He did say in effect, "No, Paul, I am not going to take away the thorn, but I am going to give you more grace and power so that you can bear it." And Paul, great man that he was, said, "Thank You, Lord. I'd rather have the thorn with Your added grace than to be without the thorn and not have Your grace."

I. We Grow Through Hard Knocks

Two couples marry. One couple has everything they need without even having to work for it. The other couple has a hard time climbing up the ladder of life. The couple who has the hard time will have the greater chance of a successful marriage. Their hard knocks will bring them closer together and make them strong.

Our country became the great nation it is because of the "hard knocks." When the early settlers arrived, they did not find an easy life. They had many hardships and struggles. It was a constant battle just to exist. But in their work and hard knocks they laid the foundation for what we enjoy today.

God's servants grow in the same way. Often the growing process nearly kills us, but it always turns out to be for our good. A young man who had been reared in the lap of luxury is called into the ministry. Without any experience he is thrown into the midst of the battle. He is called upon to serve a congregation of human beings, imperfect human beings, who are far from being the devoted Christians they ought to be. He does his best but is not of much help to anyone. As the years go by, the world crushes him and people disappoint and hurt him. Sorrows and troubles come. But these things make a sympathetic minister of him, and in time the rough edges are worn away and he becomes a blessing and help to his people. The hard knocks make him.

At a party one day a pretty young woman said, "I am so happy. I have a thousand friends." Ah, young lady, you have a great disappointment in store for you. You won't go far down the road of life until you find you have just a few true friends left. But God uses these disappointments to make us fit to serve Him and others.

If our early churches had started as magnificent temples, they would have perished. But the early Christians had to hide in caves and secret places of the earth. They were hounded by their enemies, and many of them gave up their lives for their faith. They were persecuted and "scattered." But they grew stronger and more faithful because of these hardships.

Our churches are strong today because of the bitter experiences through which they have passed. It takes these things to make us. Maybe if our churches didn't have it so easy, maybe if they were persecuted on every side, they would become stronger institutions.

II. LOOK AT SOME OF THE HARD KNOCKS

1. *There is the hard knock of failure.* A man said to me, "There are so many things I wanted and planned to do. But I am an old man now and it is too late. I feel that my life has been a failure." But sometimes these failures bring success. It is said that Edison failed dozens of times before he invented the electric light bulb. His failures spurred him on to greater efforts.

Sidney Lanier, the great Georgia poet, died at thirty, saying, "I have a thousand unwritten songs in my heart." But that sense of incompleteness had driven him to write some of the finest poems in the English language.

A certain man worked eighteen years at the same job. An opening occurred above him and he thought surely he would get a promotion. But he was passed over, and the promotion was given to someone else. He brooded over it until his mind cracked and he was placed in an institution. Failure had broken him — it is one of life's hard knocks.

2. *There is the hard knock of disappointment.* Moses had a dream. God had appointed him to lead the children of Israel to the Promised Land. But Moses failed God on one occasion, so one day God led him to the top of a high mountain where he could look down on the Land of Promise. It was such a beautiful land that Moses longed to go into it with all his heart. He

strained his eyes as he gazed upon it. He was simply aching to lead his people in. But God said, "No, Moses, you disobeyed Me in the wilderness and you'll not have the privilege of leading them. You are not going to live." Old Moses was broken-hearted; his life's dream was shattered. He must have wept many bitter tears.

How often our dreams are shattered when disappointments come. For years we look forward to some happy occurrence; it never comes, and sadness fills our hearts.

3. *There is the hard knock of bad health.* When God made man, He gave him a wonderful body; but man fell into sin, and disease and sickness set their hold upon him. When Jesus comes we'll have no sickness and He will give us perfect bodies, but now bad health seems a part of our education. In sickness we often learn the lessons of patience, sympathy, faith, and courage.

I have had some hard knocks of this kind. My body has never been very strong, and I have been in the hospital several times. I have suffered greatly, and many nights I could not sleep. Often I would get up and sit almost all night in a big chair. Some of the pain would be relieved. I have sometimes been at the point where I would ask the Lord to take me home with Him where there is no suffering. But I can truly testify that in all these moments He has been right by my side, assuring me that "all things work together for good to them who love Him."

Lou Gehrig was the star first baseman of the New York Yankees. He played in more consecutive games than any player in the history of baseball. But a dread disease set itself upon him. He could hardly bend down and tie his shoe, but he kept on playing. He never complained but soon had to drop out of baseball. The fans gave him a "Lou Gehrig Appreciation Day," and 61,000 turned out. The mayor gave him a small job on the parole board, but not long after, on June 2, 1941, he died. The manner in which he took his hard knocks won him the admiration of all America. They made a picture of his life and called it, "The Pride of the Yankees." One of my friends who saw the picture testified afterwards that it inspired him to be a better and more faithful man.

Some of the finest Christians in the world have grown spiritually because of bad health. They would never have had the influence for God that they had if they hadn't lost their health. It brought them closer to Him.

4. *There is the hard knock of deception.* You trust a friend and feel that he is on your side, but he proves untrue. Think of those sad words in the Bible, "I was wounded in the house of my friends" (Zech. 13:6). Some people put on the facade of being your best friends, but when they are away from you, they are your enemies. But Christians should never knowingly hurt anyone.

5. *There is the hard knock of persecution.* Here is a woman who wants to go to church and serve the Lord, but her husband ridicules her and even forbids her to go to God's house. Or here is a man whose wife is worldly and who nags him about the work he tries to do for the Lord. He does his best, but he is always handicapped at home. Some people are persecuted by friends or relatives. They aren't placed on the rack or the whipping post, but they are persecuted just the same.

But what did Jesus say? "Blessed are ye, when men shall revile you, and persecute you, and shall say all manner of evil against you falsely, for my sake" (Matt. 5:11).

6. *There is the hard knock of losing a loved one.* Sorrow comes and we go deep down into the valley. We feel that we cannot go on, but we are learning. The great lessons of life are not learned at a picnic. Ecclesiastes 7:2 tells us, "It is better to go to the house of mourning, than to go to the house of feasting."

> I walked a mile with Pleasure,
> She chatted all the way,
> But left me none the wiser
> For all she had to say.
>
> I walked a mile with sorrow
> And ne'er a word said she,
> But, ah, the things I learned from her,
> When Sorrow walked with me.

III. WHAT DO THESE KNOCKS DO FOR US?

We are going to the University of Hard Knocks. Are we getting any benefits from it? Yes.

1. *Hard knocks toughen us.* They train us not to be so thin-skinned. The way to ruin a child's future is to shield him from every danger. Soon he goes out into the world and life knocks him down. The person who gets a few knocks when he is young is better able to cope with life. The underprivileged child, who must wear old clothes and who learns to work, becomes more able to meet life than the one who has had everything given to him.

John Fox wrote *The Little Shepherd of Kingdom Come:* Chad and his mother lived with a surly uncle who despised both Chad and his dog, but there was no open persecution because of Chad's mother. When she died, Chad knew that trouble would come. So he took his rifle and his dog and left home. In the woods he prayed, "O God, I ain't nothing but a boy, but I must act like a man now. Help me." He faced all the storms of life and became the greatest character in the hills, a blessing to everyone. His hard life toughened him.

2. *These hard knocks teach us.* There is no hope for a man who goes through the troubles of life and learns nothing from them. Some of the biggest men in life were once failures. But they learned lessons from these failures which made them great. Experience is the greatest teacher in the world, but her lessons are the hardest.

3. *These hard knocks tenderize us.* Selfishness and pride must be knocked out before we can help others. We must be tenderized. Hard knocks make us grateful and fit us to sympathize with others.

IV. SOME GRADUATES OF THE UNIVERSITY OF HARD KNOCKS

We always measure schools by their products.

1. *Job* lost his property, his children, his health. But he said, "Though he slay me, yet will I trust him." And he came out a bigger and better man.

2. *David's* life was full of persecution and his enemies often tried to kill him. He said, "There is but a step between me and death." But through it all he could say, "The Lord is my shepherd." And he became a great king.

3. *Daniel* had the courage to say no. He kept on praying and

was finally thrown to the lions, but he came out victorious.

4. *Paul* was thrown out by his fellow Pharisees after his conversion. He was beaten, stoned, left for dead, even shipwrecked. But he said, "None of these things move me. I know that all things work together for good."

5. *John Bunyan* preached Christ and was put in jail for twelve years. But he wrote a book, *Pilgrim's Progress*, that has taken its place next to the Bible in influence.

6. *David Livingstone* labored in a factory from six A.M. to nightfall. He studied every night. Eventually God led him to Africa, where he suffered greatly. But before he died he had opened up a continent to Christ. And when he died he was highly honored. His heart was buried in Africa and his body in Westminster Abbey among some of the greatest men of the world.

Millions have lived and died and been forgotten, but others are remembered because they went through great troubles and emerged victorious people, and a blessing to others.

7. Of course, there is *Jesus*, the greatest of them all. He was despised and ridiculed. He was vilified and beaten, cursed and crucified. But He came through it all and today has a "name that is above every name."

What does all this mean to us? It means we are to go ahead in spite of the hard knocks. And we are to remember that God's grace will always be sufficient. He'll always be with us. The Christian life does not offer a downy couch and a bed of roses. But the blessed Savior will walk with us when troubles come, and He will meet us at the end of the way.

A preacher's phone rang and a girl told him, "Mother is dying, can you come?" The preacher went to the home and sat by the bedside. He quoted Psalm 23, and when he came to the words, "Yea, though I walk through the valley of the shadow of death," the woman's hand tightened on his and she said, "Wait, He is there now. I know He is with me. Go and tell the world He keeps His promise."

That's our comfort in life and in death. Regardless of what comes, He will be with us even as He promised.

6

MEETING OUR SINS AGAIN

Genesis 42:21

Many people today have reversed their thinking about God. Once they thought of Him as almighty and just, a God who punished sin. But not all people feel that way today. God is looked upon as a soft and sentimental old grandfather, a Santa Claus ready to drop all that we want into our laps if we just think positively and pray a little.

These modern thinkers are wrong. God is the same as He has always been. He has some irrevocable laws, and if we break them we will be punished. You can sin and think God has forgotten all about it, but someday you'll be forced to "meet them again" and pay the price He demands.

In Shakespeare's *Macbeth,* the title character orders his henchmen to kill Banquo. Macbeth thinks Banquo is now out of the way; but when he comes to the banquet table, he looks over at Banquo's chair and there sits Banquo's ghost. Macbeth falls back in horror. Others see the ghost but do not understand Macbeth's reaction. But Macbeth understands. He knows that he is meeting his sins again. So we have a saying today, "Banquo's ghost will not down." We mean that someday we will meet our sins again.

A farmer wrote this letter to the editor of a paper: "I planted my crop on Sunday; I worked it on Sunday; I gathered my harvest on Sunday. Yet my crop was just as good as those who go to church on Sunday. Now how do you account for that?" And the editor, who was a Christian, answered, "God does not always pay off on October first." He was simply saying, "Someday we'll meet our sins again."

Jacob had twelve sons but loved Joseph best of all. He made a coat of many colors for him and sent him into the field to see how his brothers were faring. When the jealous brothers saw him coming, they said, "Behold this dreamer cometh." In their hatred for Joseph, they threw him into a pit and later sold him into slavery. Then one of the brethren dipped Joseph's coat in blood and took it to their father, telling him that a wild animal had killed Joseph. The news broke the old man's heart, and he said, "I will go down to my grave mourning for my son."

But Joseph was not dead. He was alive down in Egypt, and after passing through many trials he finally became prime minister of Egypt, with power and authority next to that of the king himself. The famine grew worse and Jacob sent the other sons down into Egypt to buy corn. They stood before Joseph and he remembered them, but they did not know him. At first Joseph spoke roughly to them. Then he made them a proposition, "One of you go back home and bring your youngest brother, Benjamin, to me to prove the sincerity of your mission."

They knew then that they were in trouble. Since Jacob thought he had lost one son, they were reluctant to take another one from him. So they talked it over and decided to do what Joseph had suggested, saying one to another, "We are verily guilty concerning our brother. He cried out unto us but we ignored him and thus broke our father's heart. That is why this distress has come upon us." They were simply saying, "We sinned against our brother and now we are meeting our sins again." It is a warning to us: "Be sure your sin will find you out" (Num. 32:23).

I. We Always Meet Our Sins Again

One day Moses came upon two men who were fighting — an Egyptian and an Israelite. He killed and buried the Egyptian. The next day an Egyptian came up to him and said, "Are you going to kill us as you did the man yesterday?" Moses knew his sin had been discovered. When the news got back to Pharaoh, Moses had to flee for his life. He went into the land of Midian, where he dwelt for forty years. He had met his sins again.

Later God called Moses to lead Israel to the Promised Land, and Moses was faithful to that task throughout the years. Then one day God took Moses to the top of Mount Pisgah and told him that because of his disobedience at one point he would not have the privilege of leading Israel into the Promised Land. Moses died there in the land of Moab. He never had the privilege of leading the Israelites into the Promised Land, something he had dreamed about all those years. When God said, "You will not enter the land," Moses realized he was meeting his sins again.

Another great man, David, saw a beautiful woman whom he desired. He took her for himself and ordered her husband put to death. A baby was born out of this illicit union. David loved that baby very much, but in spite of all that could be done, the baby became sick and died. David's heart was broken, but he knew he was meeting his sins again. David's sons followed their father in immorality, and finally his favorite, Absalom, was killed. And in all literature there is nothing sadder than David's lament over Absalom's death (see 2 Sam. 18:33). But he couldn't escape the truth that he was meeting his sins again.

Samson was God's strong man, but he entered into sin with Delilah and gave away the secret of the source of his strength. He was captured by his enemies and put in prison. With red-hot irons they put out both of his eyes. As he ground in the mill like a common slave, the once-proud warrior must have sobbed, "I'm meeting my sins again."

When the Israelites entered Canaan, God gave them a warning. If they forgot Him and went into idolatry, He told them that He would punish them. They did forget Him and they did go into idolatry — God kept His word. He sent cruel enemies into the land, and the Israelites were carried into captivity, where they suffered for many years. As they mourned for Jerusalem in a foreign land, they must have said, "We're meeting our sins again."

King Herod killed James and threw Peter into prison. In his pride Herod made a speech and the people said, "He's a god." When Herod did not give the glory to God, in a few minutes he fell over dead and was eaten by worms. He was meeting his sins again.

A man in New York City committed a crime. He fled the state and changed his name. Many years passed and he became rich. He went back to New York, bought a fine house, and settled down to enjoy life. Then one day the officers came to that home, arrested him, and took him to prison. The years had gone by and he was meeting his sins again.

II. What Happens When We Meet Our Sins Again

1. *We remember them vividly.* Joseph's brothers did not expect trouble. They had money to buy grain and their future was bright. But when they were thrown into prison, their memory began to work. What did they remember? They remembered their sin and the pleas of Joseph. They said, "We remember the anguished look on his face when we left him in the pit and again when we sold him into slavery. That's why this trouble has come upon us."

A man who had been rescued from drowning said that in the last moments of consciousness before his rescue, the deeds of his lifetime came trooping before him. The sins he thought he had forgotten stared him in the face once more.

A man paints a picture, showing mountains and trees and rivers. Time will destroy the picture; the colors will fade. But sin paints a picture on the mind which is never destroyed. In the hour of crisis, memory brings it back.

A lunatic had been in an asylum for years. One day he escaped, and they found him at a deserted coal mine. He was looking down the shaft and crying out, "My God, down he goes." They thought this was just the ravings of a distorted mind; but when they looked down into the shaft, they found the skeleton of a man who had disappeared years before. The other man had killed him and thrown him down the shaft. The crazy man had lost his reason, but his memory was intact. Time had not dimmed the horrible picture in his mind.

Memory can curse or bless through the years. An old couple sat by the fire on a wintry night. They didn't have to talk; each knew what the other one was thinking about. They thought about how they had started out together, how they had reared their children in the admonition of God, and how near God had been to them in the hours of sorrow. They were close to heaven as they remembered their lives of goodness and service.

By contrast, an old man lay dying. He had lived for sin and the world and had rejected Christ. Memory began to work. He thought of the boy he started on the road to ruin, of the girl he had seduced. He thought of the lies he had told, the shady deals he had maneuvered. All of a sudden the room was filled with devils and the shrieks of a man going down to death without Christ. His memories were as the fires of hell.

Every day we hang pictures on the walls of memory. They are either good or bad. Someday every sin, evil deed, and thought will come to memory again.

2. *Our consciences accuse us of guilt.* "A guilty conscience needs no accuser." Our consciences bring our sins before us again. Lady Macbeth looked at her lily-white hands and cried out, "Here's the smell of blood still; all the perfumes of Arabia will not sweeten this little hand." There wasn't any blood on her hands. The stains were on her conscience.

Ahab killed Naboth and took his vineyard for himself. But later when Ahab met the prophet Elijah in the same vineyard, Ahab cried out, "Hast thou found me, oh mine enemy?" Why did he call the prophet his enemy? Hadn't they parted as friends? When Ahab saw the prophet, his conscience smote him.

There are people in our churches who were once faithful and active. Now they have turned to sin and worldliness. When you ask them why they quit going to church, they blame it on the preacher or someone else.

3. *Our reason condemns us through the Holy Spirit.* You look back over your days and you remember certain sins. Your conscience smites you, and you say, "I had it coming to me." Like the brothers of Joseph you say, "I know now why all of this distress has come upon me."

What did the dying thief on the cross say? He said, "We are receiving the due reward for our deeds." The Bible tells us that every sin will be punished. Reason says that when we have sinned, we are guilty and deserve to be punished.

But you say, "I know men who sin and get away with it. They are not punished." David felt the same way. He said, "The wicked prosper and nothing happens to them. I live a good life and still suffer. They have all they want, but God whips me every day." Then he said that he went to church, and God caused him to understand. He came to know that God does not always punish the wicked here on earth, but has hell reserved for them. He said that their feet would slide in due time, but that God would take care of him.

III. THE ONLY REMEDY FOR SIN

As the brothers of Joseph fell before him in confession, so we are to fall at Jesus' feet and confess and forsake our sins. A physican examines a sick man and tells him that he has an incurable disease. He offers no remedy; he renders no service. But Jesus, the Great Physician, offers Himself as a remedy for sin. "The blood of Christ cleanses from all sin. . . . Him that cometh to me I will not cast out. . . . Though your sins be as scarlet they shall be as white as snow." The only way to get rid of sin is to come to the "fountain filled with blood."

A certain physician always smiled when he entered a patient's room. Someone said, "How can you live in the midst of all of this suffering and not be overwhelmed?" He replied, "I always look upon disease and suffering from the curative standpoint." Jesus looks at it in the same way. He can heal us of sin when we come to Him.

The *Titanic* was the greatest ship built in her day. Captain Smith took her out on her maiden voyage. She was a floating palace, a thing of beauty. Some of the world's richest and most prominent people were on board. On Sunday night some icebergs were sighted, but no one was afraid. They knew the *Titanic* was unsinkable. The bar was open, and the passengers were drinking and dancing. A small group of Christians was on board. At 9:30 P.M. the band stopped playing for intermission. One man went out on the dance floor and announced, "Some of us are Christians. We have with us a Bible and some

Meeting Our Sins Again

songbooks. I don't want to preach to you, but just to read a passage and sing a hymn. After all, this is the Lord's Day, and we ought to honor it." A man in the crowd cried out, "To hell with all that. Get out of here."

In a few minutes there was a crash, but the passengers thought nothing of it, for the *Titanic* was unsinkable. Then came the cry, "The ship is sinking," and the band played, "Nearer My God to Thee." Many people fell on their knees and cried out to the God they had previously blasphemed. Some were rescued, but hundreds went down to a watery grave. They cried out to God, but without genuine faith their cry was in vain.

Some of you have no place in your life for Christ, the Bible, or the church. Eventually your sins will meet you again at Judgment Day and damn you forever. There is one way to avoid this. Come in repentance and faith to Jesus and let Him save you.

7

BEHOLD THE MAN

John 19:1-6

It is natural for us to have a desire to see great men in person. If the president of our country came to our city, we would crowd the streets to get a glimpse of him. We greet those who are prominent with curiosity and admiration. We should be just as eager to see the greatest Man of all, the God-Man, the Lord Jesus Christ.

As we look at the text, we see Jesus in the hands of Pilate. He has been scourged and spat upon, and a crown of thorns has been jammed on His head. All kinds of cruelties and insults have been heaped on Him. Now Pilate brings Him out onto the balcony. A great crowd has gathered in the courtyard below. Pilate cries out to them, "Behold the man." And the answer comes ringing back, "Crucify him, crucify him!"

Today I stand in Pilate's place, and I say to each of you, "Behold the Man! Look upon the One who was wounded for your transgressions and bruised for your iniquities, who bore your griefs and carried your sorrows, who was crucified in your stead." Do you get tired of a preacher talking about Jesus? I would rather say the same thing over and over about Jesus than something new about someone else. Jesus is the preacher's theme. Every message should center around the person of Jesus Christ.

Take Christ out of a sermon and you've taken the heart out of it. A Christless sermon is a joy to hell and a sorrow to heaven. It wastes the time of men and endangers their souls. You can't get too much of Christ — Christ in prophecy, Christ in the manger, Christ on the cross, Christ in the tomb, Christ risen and ascended, Christ on the throne, Christ coming again. So come today and behold the Man.

I. BEHOLD THE MAN TO RECEIVE KNOWLEDGE

There are some things we learn at Calvary that we can learn nowhere else.

1. *At Calvary we learn the evil nature of sin.* We can see it in a thousand pictures. Look at the Garden of Eden, once the most beautiful spot in all the world, now bare and desolate. Sin did that. Look at the heavenly pair, Adam and Eve, driven out of Eden, digging their living out of the soil. Sin did that. Look at the Flood, with men and women and children shrieking and going down to death. Sin did that. Look at Sodom and Gomorrah, covered with fire and brimstone. Sin did that. Look at the multitude of Egyptians lying dead in the Red Sea. Sin did that. What brought sickness and trouble into the world? Sin. What brought death to take our loved ones away? Sin. What blasts and breaks and ruins life? Sin. What built hell and the regions of the damned? Sin.

But all this is nothing compared to the worst thing sin ever did. It put God's Son to death. Our sin fashioned His cross, drove the nails into His hands and feet, pressed the crown down on His brow, and thrust the sword in His side. It brought forth the cry, "My God, my God, why hast thou forsaken me?"

In the Highland Valley of Scotland there is a great stone with grass growing around its base. Years ago this stone hung on a precipice overlooking the valley. One day as a shepherd walked beneath the stone, it fell on him and crushed him. Behold the Man, Christ Jesus! On the cross our sin fell on Him and crushed Him to death. At Calvary we learn something of the evil nature of our sin.

2. *At Calvary we learn the sureness of God's justice.* Someone may say, "God can do all things. Why doesn't He just pass over our sins instead of demanding a sacrifice?" Well, God is a God of justice, and a just judge never says, "It's nothing; just forget your crime." Neither can a just God overlook our sin. Every sin must be punished; that punishment must fall on the

sinner or on someone in his stead. And Jesus loved us so much that He became the One who suffered in our place.

Brutus of old passed certain laws and decreed that if anyone should break one of these laws, he should be killed. To his great sorrow his own son was the first person to break one of his laws. "Surely you will spare your own son," his courtiers said. "No," said Brutus, "he has broken the law of his country and he must die."

God's law says, "The soul that sinneth, it shall die" (Ezek. 18:4). We have sinned and we deserved to die, but Jesus took our sins upon Himself. "He that spared not his own Son, but delivered him up for us all, how shall he not with him also freely give us all things?" (Rom. 8:32).

Jesus had no sin, but sin was imputed to Him. But our sins are our own actual sins. If God punished His own Son who bore only imputed sins, surely He will punish us for our actual sins unless we come with them to the Christ who died for us.

Here is a great text in Hebrews 2:3: "How shall we escape, if we neglect so great salvation?" If we go through life without a Savior, if we have no one to bear our sin, God's justice will be carried out and His wrath will fall upon us.

3. *At Calvary we learn the greatness of God's love.* Our entire world is an expression of God's love. If we could read the stars rightly, they would spell *love*. If we could interpret the language of the storms, it would spell *love*. If we could gather all the flowers together, they would spell *love*. All the world speaks of God's love, but if you would know the depths of it you must "behold the Man."

In time of war young men are called to serve. The only son of a widow decided to enlist. His mother said, "It's the right thing, the only thing to do." She sent him away with a smile, not knowing if he would ever come back. Then she went into the house, closed the door, and wept. She had given her best, but even that was as nothing to compare with God's love. He sent down His Son to certain death, and it broke His heart. He did all this because He loved us.

When I was a boy, I would often take a sea shell and hold it to my ear. In it I could hear the faraway whisper of the sea. God's blessings are all around us, and as we think of them, they whisper to us of His love. But when we go to Calvary and "behold the Man," the greatness of His love is trumpeted to us.

II. Behold the Man to Feel Emotions

When you see a play and watch the audience, you notice that they are moved by various emotions — joy, sorrow, boredom. But what happened at Calvary was no play; it was grim tragedy. What should be our feelings as we "behold the Man"?

1. *This view ought to make us sorrowful.* We seek happiness, but the time comes for sorrow over our sin. If we have never known spiritual sorrow, we have never known spiritual joy. If we have never shed penitential tears, we have never sung heavenly joy.

Oh, that you and I might weep over our sins at the feet of Jesus. We did that when we were first converted, but now we sin and feel no penitence because of it. Oh, how we need to probe our hearts, search out our sins, and come weeping in repentance to the foot of the cross.

> Alas, and did my Savior bleed?
> And did my Sov'reign die?
> Would He devote that sacred head
> For such a worm as I?

Did He die for you and me? Yes. Did we slay Him? Yes. If we had accidentally killed our best friend, we would mourn over it the rest of our lives. And since we slew the Son of God, we ought to view His death with the greatest sorrow. Shall we ever see a cross without shedding a tear? Shall we ever hear of Calvary without being plunged into sorrow? Shall we ever hear the name of the Crucified One without deep grief?

> But drops of grief can ne'er repay
> The debt of love I owe:
> Here, Lord, I give myself away,
> 'Tis all that I can do!

2. *This view ought to make us happy.* "Behold the Man" and let that view bring us the greatest joy. Alice Freeman Palmer taught a summer school for poor children in Boston. The women from the slums left their children with her while they

were at work. One day she asked a group of mothers this question, "What shall I tell your children?" And they replied, "Tell them how to be happy." This is the cry of all humanity, "Where shall we find happiness?" And here is the answer, "Come to the cross and behold the Man."

Christ makes us happy, and the more we have of Him, the happier we'll be. There are some who have so little true religion that they go out searching for happiness in the world. But they don't find it there. They have too much of the world in them to make them happy in the Spirit, and just enough true religion in them to make them unhappy in the world.

One man says, "Eat, drink, and be merry, and you'll be happy." But happiness is not found in that kind of life. The lustful man satisfies every passion and doesn't find happiness there. The dissipated man drinks the dregs of life and is miserable. The ambitious man climbs the ladder of success and is disappointed. But "behold the Man." You'll find happiness in Him.

3. *This view ought to make us love Him.* As we behold Jesus, we should say, "Oh, how I love Him." Robert Browning, the great English poet, loved Italy, where he and his wife lived for fifteen years. In one of his poems he says, "Open my heart and you will see, /'graved inside of it, 'Italy.'" And if our hearts were opened, people should see on the inside the matchless name of Jesus engraved upon it.

How can we come to love Jesus? Just by walking with Him, that's all. The more we live with Him, the more we love Him. Some of us are so unlovely that it's enough to see us once every ten years. But others are so lovely we want to see them every minute. It's that way with Jesus. If we could have walked the Judean hills with Him, surely we would have loved Him. We can't walk with Him in the flesh every day, but we can walk with Him in the Spirit at all times.

Ignatius was brought to the Roman Colosseum and called upon to curse God or die. He replied, "These many years have I served Him and He never did me a displeasure. I cannot curse Him, but I can die for Him." Oh, that we loved Him like that!

My Jesus, I love Thee, I know Thou art mine,
For Thee all the follies of sin I resign;
My gracious Redeemer, my Savior art Thou;
If ever I loved Thee, my Jesus, 'tis now.

III. BEHOLD THE MAN TO MAKE HOLY RESOLUTIONS

1. *The Christian should resolve to live a better life.* The true pastor is greatly concerned over his people who are living for the world and not for Christ. If we could get our members to "behold the Man" in the right way, surely they would go out to live a better life for Him. I believe if I had the power to take you back to that day when He died on the cross and have you watch Him bleed His life away for you, the world would lose its charm for you. You would never be the same again.

Oh, the sins of those who profess to belong to Christ! They are not always guilty of the gross sins of the flesh, but their hearts and lives are filled with worldliness, covetousness, pettiness, malice, jealousy, and other things that prevent them from being the Christians they should be. Do not tell me that you love Jesus, while you continue to live in sin.

The Persians have a pertinent fable. A man picked up a piece of scented clay. "Oh, clay," he said, "where did you get your pleasant perfume?" And the clay answered, "Once I was just a piece of common clay, then I was laid for a time by a rose and I drank of its fragrance. Since then I have never lost my aroma." Now if we just live close to Jesus and let Him fill our hearts with the sweetness of His personality, our lives will influence others with sweetness and goodness.

2. *The lost person should resolve to give himself to Jesus.* There is salvation in Him alone — you can look unto Him and live. You may attend church regularly, you may love the fellowship of Christian people, but you are on the road to eternal hell if you hold onto your sin and ignore Jesus. If you will just get the proper look at Jesus, you will want to say good-by to your sin.

A deep-sea diver who was a devout Christian had a sea shell on his mantel, with a piece of paper caught in the shell. In telling the story of that shell he said, "One day I was at the bottom of the sea when I saw that shell with a piece of paper in it. I took the paper out and found that it was a tract inviting sinners to Jesus. Since God's mercy had followed me to the bottom of the sea, I felt I could hold out no longer against Him. So I gave my heart to Him." God has been pursuing some of you year after year. Why not yield to Him?

The Lambs Club was composed of the most prominent men in London. In one of their meetings they talked of the great persons they wished they had known: Chaucer, Shakespeare, and many others. One noted man said, "If one of these men came into this room, what would you do?" And another answered, "I would bow down in respect and admiration before him." Another one said, "But if Jesus came in, what would you do?" And the answer came back, "I would fall in homage at His feet like Thomas did and cry out, 'My Lord and my God.'"

As we behold Him today, may we say the same. "My Lord and my God, I'll follow Thee to the end of the way."

8

PRECIOUS IN THE SIGHT OF THE LORD

Psalm 116:15

The Bible has much to say about the death of Christians. The trouble with us is that we either neglect or don't believe those great truths. We think of death as the end of all things good, as a separation from everyone and everything we love. We think of death as a hideous monster who has come to cut us off from all our joys.

But really, death for a Christian is a wonderful thing. Suppose you were in a prison camp where you were persecuted and beaten every day, where they drove bamboo shoots under your nails, where they gave you nothing to eat but stale bread, where you were forced to sleep on the cold ground. Then suppose some friends came in and rescued you and took you to a place of rest and gave you good food and brought you happiness. Wouldn't you consider your rescuers as good friends?

Well, we ought to look upon death in that way. We live in a cruel world. There are a few joys down here, but many hardships and injustices, trials and tears, sorrows and separations. When death comes, we are taken into the presence of the Lord, to the land of eternal sunshine, to a place of perfect health and perfect rest. Wouldn't you say that death is a good friend, one of God's servants to take you to a better land?

Someone pictured death in this way: A little child is playing late in the evening with some children. They mistreat him and abuse him. He becomes weary and sick at heart. Then a kind nurse comes and takes him home. She places him in bed, tucks the covers around him, and soon he drifts off into peaceful slumber. Death is that kind nurse. God sends him down to snatch us away from the hardships of life and give us eternal rest.

Listen to what the Bible says about death: "Blessed are the dead which die in the Lord from henceforth: Yea, saith the Spirit, that they may rest from their labours; and their works do follow them" (Rev. 14:13); "Absent from the body, . . . present with the Lord" (2 Cor. 5:8); "He giveth his beloved sleep" (Ps. 127:2); and "For me to live is Christ, and to die is gain" (Phil. 1:21).

Listen to Paul as he approaches death: "I have fought a good fight, I have finished my course, I have kept the faith: henceforth there is laid up for me a crown of righteousness, which the Lord, the righteous judge, shall give me at that day: and not to me only, but unto all them also that love his appearing" (2 Tim. 4:7, 8).

I am not saying that death is a pretty thing. It hurts us to stand by and see our loved ones suffer and die. Yet remember this: While our own hearts are breaking, our loved ones have gone up to meet Jesus and to receive all the wonderful things He has in store for them.

Now we come to this wonderful text, "Precious in the sight of the LORD is the death of his saints" (Ps. 116:15). When a Christian dies, it is not a matter of indifference to the Lord. He knows about every pain, every breath that is drawn, every groan that is uttered. All of it means something to Him. The text does not say that death is precious in our sight, but in God's sight. It speaks of death from God's viewpoint.

A young preacher married a fine girl, but within three months she died. The preacher who conducted the funeral quoted Romans 8:28. The young preacher said, "I know that's in the Bible, but I can't see how it's true in my case." He was looking at the matter from a human standpoint and not from God's.

In 1973 my eldest son died. It seemed that he had everything to live for when God took him. I do not understand it because I look at it from the human viewpoint. But if I could see it from God's viewpoint, I know I would see it was for the best.

Whether in war or peace, whether death comes suddenly or after a lingering illness, whether on a busy highway or in a quiet bedroom, I believe it comes because God permits it and that it is precious in His sight.

I. The Death of a Child of God Means a Change of Environment

We live in an environment of sin. The best Christian is surrounded by it; the best home is contaminated by it. On every hand there is sin in some form. Every form of sin characterizes our environment. But in heaven there is a complete change. No more do we rub elbows with dishonesty, drunkenness, lies, lust, or any other sin. Instead of being surrounded by sinners, we associate with the angels, with the redeemed of all ages, and with the Lord Jesus Christ Himself.

Think of the by-products of sin: sickness, sorrow, pain, poverty, broken hearts and homes, death. These came into the world because of sin. But when God's people die, they go to a place where there is never any sickness, sorrow, trouble, or pain. No more operations, no more weeping, no more funerals. No wonder a Christian's death is precious in God's sight. He knows that person is safe from all these things.

There is an old, old debate that has never been settled, "Which is stronger, heredity or environment?" I believe environment is the stronger. Take a child from ungodly parents when he is one day old, give him to Christian parents, let them bring him up in a godly home, and I believe he will probably become more good than bad. But take a child from a Christian couple when he is one day old, give him to a godless, drunken, profane couple, and let them bring him up in that atmosphere. I am sure he will more probably turn out bad rather than good. Yes, environment is a mighty power, because we live in a world where the devil is so active, where sin and its by-products press down upon us.

But what a change when we get to heaven! We go from sin to sinlessness, from earth's hovels to heaven's mansions, from earth's discords to heaven's harmony, from all that is bad to all that is good, from all that hurts to all that brings happiness. No wonder the death of a saint, a child of God, is precious in God's sight.

When Sir Walter Raleigh was put to death, he was as serene and calm as a June morning. Running his finger over the axe to be used in beheading him, he said, "This is a sharp medic but it is a cure for all diseases." Yes, death cures all our diseases and changes our environment from gloom to glory.

II. The Death of a Child of God Means a Change of Nature

In this life we are all burdened with a carnal, sinful, fleshly nature. It causes us continual grief; it is always getting us into trouble. We don't want to sin — that's the spiritual nature within us. But we do go ahead and sin — that's the old carnal nature within us.

Simon Peter loved Jesus, but one night he lied. He said he didn't know Jesus, and he punctuated his denial with an oath. Then Jesus looked at him and that one look broke Peter's heart. He went out and wept bitterly. His denial was a result of his carnal or sinful nature, which was always a burden to him. Paul was the great apostle, but he said, "The things I want to do, I do not; the things I ought not to do, I do." He said it was because of the sinful nature that dwelt within him.

David was a man after God's own heart, but he sinned greatly. When he repented, he said that God was breaking his bones. David did not mean this literally — he was using a figure of speech. He really meant he was as miserable as if all his bones were broken. He had allowed his old carnal nature to get the upper hand.

This is the experience of every Christian. We know Christ, and deep down in our hearts we want to be good and do good. But that old sinful nature is still with us. It drags us down, makes us weep, and becomes a burden to us.

But when we die there is a change of nature. The old nature is gone forever. As the song says:

> This robe of flesh I'll drop and rise
> To seize the everlasting prize.

It will be wonderful when there is nothing in us to drag us down and make us do and say evil things. We'll be like that when we meet Jesus. Whether we die or are caught up in the air, the results will be the same. Whether we go by the undertaker or the "uppertaker," we'll leave our old, sinful, carnal, fleshly natures behind.

III. THE DEATH OF A CHILD OF GOD PROVES THE REALITY OF OUR RELIGION

Some Christians live in such a way that the world doubts the reality of their religion. But when a true Christian dies, he testifies to the presence and reality of religion. The Lord is never quite so close as in the hour of death. John Wesley said, "Our people die well." He was simply saying that Christ is real in that hour.

Stephen was stoned to death. While Paul watched over the cloaks of the stoners, he heard Stephen say, "Lord, lay not this sin to their charge." Paul never forgot Stephen's words and his attitude. They prepared him for his conversion. He must have said, "If a man can die like that, there must be something to the Christian religion."

Polycarp was a great Christian in the early church. He was condemned to die by burning, but was promised his life if he would renounce Christ. He said, "Eighty and six years have I served Him and He has never wronged me. How can I forsake Him now?" They burned his body, but his soul went to be with God. Men don't die like that unless Christianity is a reality to them.

IV. THE DEATH OF A CHILD OF GOD DRAWS CHRISTIANS NEARER TO HIM

In Numbers 23:10 we read, "Let me die the death of the righteous, and let my last end be like his!" This man had seen a godly man die and how the Lord was with him. He too wanted to die like that.

A certain man was a Christian, but not a very faithful one. One day his son, whom he loved greatly, died suddenly. The night after the funeral he began to read his Bible. He took a red pencil and marked every verse that spoke of heaven, where his son had gone. This Bible reading brought him closer to God. His son's death had drawn him closer to God.

I conducted a meeting in Athens, Georgia. On Sunday night my brother called from our old home-place. He said, "You had better come home if you want to see papa alive." I drove the twenty-four miles and sat by my father's bedside until he died the next morning. One of my brothers and I went into the next room, and through his tears my brother said, "It makes you want to live a better life, doesn't it?" And certainly it is true that when one of our loved ones goes to be with God we are brought closer to Him.

V. THE DEATH OF A CHILD OF GOD MEANS A WELCOME HOME FOR HIM

This world is not our home. The years we spend here are nothing compared to eternity. Our citizenship is in heaven, and before long we will be going to our home.

We once lived in a little town nestled among the hills of western North Carolina. Often we would go away from home, but we always looked forward to getting back. Several miles out of town we would come to the top of a hill. From it we could look down on the little town. We were always glad when we reached that spot, because it meant we were almost home. Someday on the highway of life we're going to come to that last hill, and the saints and angels and the blessed Jesus will be waiting to welcome us home.

Some years ago my wife and I took a trip to Hawaii. When the ship docked in San Francisco, hundreds of people were there to welcome their loved ones. The band was playing and many relatives and friends rushed forward to welcome their loved ones back home. But there was no one there to meet us, for we didn't know anyone in San Francisco. But it's going to be different when the old ship Zion pulls into glory. Loved ones and friends and the Savior whom we've tried to serve will be there to welcome us into the heavenly city.

A native preacher of Africa said, "When a heathen is dying, the witch doctor puts a dead bone in his hand as a passport into another land. When a Christian dies, he doesn't grasp a dead bone, but the hand of the living Lord." Yes, thank God, when we come to the end of the journey, the Lord Himself will welcome us home.

A preacher stood by the bedside of a dying saint. This godly woman called her children in one by one and told them good-by. Then she asked the preacher to read Psalm 90 and the passages in Revelation about heaven. He did so and then she said, "The angels are at the foot of the bed. They've come for me." She fell asleep to wake up in the presence of the King.

Don't you want to die like that? Don't you want to go to heaven at the end of the way? Then put your trust in the Lord Jesus Christ. Your death will be precious in God's sight, and you can say with Paul, "For me to live is Christ, and to die is gain."

9

THE LURE OF THE UPWARD LOOK

Psalm 121

Some time ago I was visiting a home in the mountains. I sat on the front porch and gazed at the beautiful panorama of mountains, sky, and clouds surrounding me. I said to the lady who lived there, "You must enjoy the view here. It is really an inspiration." She replied, "I never see it." She had lived there all her life and had become so accustomed to the view that she missed all the beauty, joy, and strength of the everlasting hills.

This was not true of the psalmist. He said, "I will lift up mine eyes unto the hills, from whence cometh my help." He meant that he was going to lift up his soul toward heaven and get a fresh glimpse of God, so that he could receive the strength only God could give.

During our lives on earth we surrender to the things that drag us down. We are buying and selling, working and playing, striving and struggling. The great danger is that our eyes will become glued on earthly things. Oh, let us remove our eyes from these things. Let us lift up the eyes of our souls and look beyond the hills toward the throne of God. All of our help must come from Him. Without Him we are weak, powerless, helpless.

God's biggest events are associated with the mountains. On Mount Ararat the ark rested after the Flood. On Mount Moriah Abraham was summoned to offer Isaac. On Mount Sinai the law was given to Moses. On Mount Carmel Elijah prayed and the fire fell. On the Mount of Transfiguration Jesus was transformed and became as light. On Mount Calvary the Son of God died for a lost world. On the Mount of Olives Jesus left His friends but told them that someday He would come back. Oh, that we might lift the eyes of our souls to the heights.

A poet said:

> Two men looked out from prison bars,
> The one saw mud, the other stars.

That's the trouble with so many of us today. We are looking down instead of looking toward the stars and the God who made them.

I. The Upward Look Brings Salvation

A saved person is one who has had a spiritual vision — he has looked up to God through faith in the Lord Jesus.

Jesus said, "As Moses lifted up the serpent in the wilderness, even so must the Son of Man be lifted up." What was He talking about? Go back into the history of Israel to find the answer. The people were on the way to the Promised Land; they had sinned against God, and God had sent judgment upon them, as He always does. He sent fiery serpents into the camp. They bit the people and many were dying. But God always provides a way of salvation. He told Moses to make a serpent of brass and to lift it high upon a pole. He was to tell the people that if they looked beyond the serpent and to God they would be healed. Imagine a man in his tent. The fiery serpent has bitten him and he is dying. Then someone tells him of the brazen serpent on the pole. He drags himself to the tent door and hears a voice saying, "Look up, look up." So the man looks away from himself and up toward God. As he does so he feels healing power entering his body, and he leaps for joy.

Now Jesus makes the application. He says, "You are dying of sin but God so loved the world that He gave His only begotten Son, that whosoever believeth in Him should not perish, but have everlasting life." And all over the world men have looked and been cleansed of sin and saved from hell.

I saw it in South America. I was invited to preach in Rio de Janeiro. That Sunday I looked out upon people I had never seen before and would never see again. They couldn't speak my language, and I couldn't speak theirs. But through an interpreter I preached on the subject "Ye Must Be Born Again." When the invitation was given, a middle-aged woman came forward weeping over her sin and surrendering to Jesus. She looked beyond the strange preacher and the language barrier and saw Jesus. She saw Him in salvation.

Some people look elsewhere for salvation. They look at their own righteousness and say, "I am better than those people in the church." But the Bible says their righteousness is but as filthy rags in God's sight. It says that by the deeds of the law no flesh is justified.

Some people look at their own goodness. They say, "I live a good clean life; I don't need Him. Christ died for vile sinners, but I am not one of them. I don't need Him." Oh, friend, you need *everything!* You're blind! You're doomed!

Some people even trust other peoples' badness. They say, "He says he is a Christian, but he's not what he ought to be." And they comfort themselves by saying that they are better than others. But there is no salvation in that. The issue is between you and God, not between you and others. Everyone must give an account of himself to God, not an account of someone else.

When we look elsewhere than to Christ, there is no hope for us. Salvation comes when we look away from sin and self to the Savior.

When Charles H. Spurgeon was sixteen years of age, he dropped into a small church on Sunday morning. The pastor was not there that morning and a layman preached a simple sermon to the twelve people in the congregation. When he came to the words "look unto Me" in his text, he pointed his finger at Spurgeon and said, "Look, young man. Look to Jesus and He will save you." The young man looked in faith to Jesus and was saved that morning. By the time he was nineteen he was preaching to greater crowds than any man in London.

Are you looking to Jesus for salvation? Is your life devoid of hope? What if tomorrow were your last day on earth? Do you shudder as you think of the judgment? Then look up to Jesus, and He'll save you. Romans 8:1 tells us that "there is therefore now no condemnation to them which are in Christ Jesus."

II. The Upward Look Brings Peace

You have heard the expression, "pouring oil on troubled waters." Man's life is just a mass of troubled waters. There is no peace on earth for him. He must lift up his eyes to find it.

A storm was raging on the sea, and the passengers on the ship were frantic with fear. Then they saw a little girl who was as calm as she could be. "Why are you so quiet?" someone asked her. "Aren't you afraid?" "No," she answered, "my father is running the ship." Is life beating you, upsetting you, troubling you? Then remember that God is your Father, that He has all power. Look up; He will not let you down.

Life is full of shadows. They fall on you and rob you of peace. There are the shadows of sickness, of grief, of doubt, of financial trouble, of the fear of old age, and of death and the hereafter. But listen, where there are shadows there must be light. And Jesus is that light. If you will put your hand in His and follow Him, you will find peace in the darkest hour. When you get the blues, when you are downhearted and discouraged, don't look down. Look up to God for peace.

III. The Upward Look Brings Strength

We are so weak. We are like the song, "I am weak but Thou art strong." There is so much to do, so many choices to be made, so many temptations to be overcome. The psalmist said, "My help cometh from the Lord." That's where we must get our help, too.

God promises strength for every day. We don't need strength now for all the days, but for today. And God says, "As thy days shall demand, so shall thy strength ever be." We don't need enough bread for a week, but just enough for today. We don't wind our watches for a week, but just for a day. So God promises to take care of us, one day at a time.

A company of men stood at the edge of a cliff. One of their number was at the bottom of the cliff, helpless. They asked a shepherd boy if he would put a rope around his waist and take it to the man below. He looked over at his strong-armed father and said, "I'll go if you'll let my father hold the rope." Let us not fear life or death. God is holding the rope and "underneath are the Everlasting Arms."

The Lure of the Upward Look

Someone asked Haydn, the great composer, how he recovered his strength after his exertions. He replied, "I have a small chapel in my home. When I am weary, I go there and pray, and God never fails me." God says, "Without me ye can do nothing." Paul said, "I can do all things through Christ who strengtheneth me."

IV. THE UPWARD LOOK BRINGS HOPE

If it were not for the sweet voice of hope whispering in our ears, we could not go on another day. How did Moses survive his trials? He had the hope of seeing Jesus one day. How did Lindbergh fly nonstop for thirty-three hours? He had the hope of finding land and fame. How did Pasteur endure so much criticism and persecution? He had the hope of making discoveries that would save lives. How does the goldminer dig on and on? He has the hope of striking a vein of gold one day. It is hope that leads us on.

We look up to God and hope fills our souls. We hope for better things when we hear Him say, "All things work together for good to them that love God." We have the hope of seeing Jesus one day. "Because I live," He said, "ye too shall live." Paul gave his soul to Jesus and therefore he could say, "I am persuaded that he is able to keep that which I have committed unto him against that day."

We have a saying, "Where there's life there's hope." Yes, if we follow Jesus, we shall have hope, and we shall live. One dark Friday as we see His dead body hanging on the cross, we say, "There's no hope for me in that dead body." But He burst the bonds of death and came back to live forever; so we say, "If He can do that, there's hope in Him for me. He overcame death and the grave so I'll look up to Him. I know He'll carry me home." Oh, hopeless heart, look up to Jesus and you'll be safe forever.

V. THE UPWARD LOOK BRINGS ACTION

As we look up to God, as we remember all He has done, is doing, and will do for us, we are bound to say, "What can I do for Him who does so much for me?" A look at Jesus will bring action on our part.

1. *There is the action of love.* We will love God. Do you remember how Zacchaeus climbed down out of the tree to see Jesus? There is a legend about Zacchaeus. It tells us that when he became an old man he would take a walk every day at sunrise. His wife became curious about it and followed him one morning. She saw him go over to the tree, water its roots, put his arms fondly around its trunk, and whisper, "This is the tree that brought me to Him whom my soul loveth." If we remember how He saved us, we cannot help but love Him with all our hearts.

And if we look up toward God, we will love others, too. A person who loves Christ cannot help but love those for whom He died. You tell me that you love the Lord, but when I learn that you don't love people I know you don't really love God.

"If a man say, I love God, and hateth his brother, he is a liar: for he that loveth not his brother whom he hath seen, how can he love God whom he hath not seen? And this commandment have we from him, That he who loveth God love his brother also" (1 John 4:20,21).

A man in the Orient had a great deal of money and much wisdom, but no peace in his heart. He wanted to die. Then a man brought him a healing herb and said, "Heal seven people and then die." He healed seven people and then was asked, "Now are you ready to die?" And he replied, "No, for now I have found the true meaning of life." The true meaning of life is serving and loving others in the name of Christ.

2. *There is the action of consecration.* If your eyes beheld the King in the right way, you would want to give yourself to Him. When Napoleon invaded Russia, he captured a woodsman who was extremely loyal to the Czar. An officer commanded that the man be shot, but the man was so calm the officer revoked the order and gave the command that the letter "N" be branded on the man's hand, standing for Napoleon. When told that the initial stood for "Napoleon," the man seized an axe and cut off his hand. "There now," he said, "there is not one part of me that does not belong to the Czar."

The Lure of the Upward Look 81

That's consecration. Has the devil put any mark on you? Is there any part of you that doesn't belong to Christ? Then cut it off and give that part of yourself to Christ.

3. *There is the action of service.* An Englishman came to the United States and asked the question, "Don't you have any gentlemen here?" "What do you mean?" he was asked. "In England," he replied, "gentlemen are people who don't work for a living." "Yes, we have many of them," answered the American, "but over here we call them tramps." There are too many tramps in the church of Christ. He needs workers.

A boy was leaving his aunt's house in the rain. He grabbed an umbrella from the rack, but his aunt quickly said, "Don't use that one. We've had it for twenty-three years, but it has never been wet. I don't want it to get wet now." Some people are that way with their talents. They have talents, but they are not using them for God. What are you good for — good for God or good for nothing?

In *Pilgrim's Progress* Christian tells Hopeful to relate his Christian experience. He answered, "Once I was a deep sinner, a drunkard, a swearing man, a Sabbath breaker. One day my sin was so heavy upon me that I looked up to heaven, I saw Jesus and gave myself to Him and was saved. Now I live a holy life and long to serve Jesus. If I had 1,000 gallons of blood in my body, I would gladly spill them all for Jesus."

Oh, beloved, wasn't it that way when you first met Jesus? Now you are too busy for Him; the world has come in, and you've lost that feeling. You need a fresh experience with God. So come today and get back in step with Jesus.

> I've wandered far away from God,
> Now I'm coming home.
> The paths of sin too long I've trod,
> Now I'm coming home.
>
> Coming home, coming home,
> Nevermore to roam.
> Open wide Thine arms of love,
> Lord, I'm coming home.

10

CHRIST MAY RETURN AT ANY MOMENT

Hebrews 10:37

The Word of God rings out with the truth that Jesus may come back at any moment. No one knows the day or the hour, but we have every reason to believe His coming is near. It could happen while you are reading this sermon. It could happen while you are in bed tonight or at work tomorrow. While the fact of His coming is a scriptural certainty, the date of His coming is uncertain. God knew it was best to withhold this fact from us.

If the glorious truth that Christ may come today gripped our hearts, it would revolutionize our lives. We would turn away from all sin, loosen our hold on the world, strip off all the nonessentials and give our very best to Jesus every day.

Here is a mother who says to her little girl, "I am going to town. If you keep your face and hands and dress clean, I'll bring you a present. I don't know exactly what time I will return." The little girl will do her best to keep clean so that she will be ready to stand the test when her mother returns. If the mother told her that she would return at three o'clock the next day, the child might not clean up until two o'clock.

So if Christ had said, "I will be coming back at such-and-such a time on a certain day," most people would probably say, "I'll wait until the day before that time to get ready." But since we don't know the date, but do know that He might come at any minute, we should be inspired to get ready. Let's quit wasting our lives on trivial things, and throwing away our time and talent and money on the things of the world. Let's give Him 100 percent in anticipation of that glad hour. Then we won't have any regrets over the past when He comes with a shout, the voice of the archangel, and the trump of God.

Now we are to remember that His coming is in two stages. He will come first in the air to raise the bodies of the dead saints from their graves, to catch up to Himself the believers who are still alive upon the earth. Then after a period of time, thought by Bible scholars to be about seven years, a time of tribulation upon the earth, He will return to the earth with all of His saints. Remember this — He comes first *for* His own; He comes next *with* His own. Right now we are looking for Him to come in the air. This could happen at any moment. His coming is imminent; it is near; it may be today.

I. JESUS SPOKE OF HIS IMMINENT COMING

1. *There is a warning in Matthew 24:44:* "Therefore be ye also ready: for in such an hour as ye think not the Son of man cometh." Jesus told us about a certain ruler who left two servants behind to look after his interests. One servant was faithful to his duties, and when his master returned suddenly, the master rewarded him. But the other servant was unfaithful — he misbehaved and got drunk. When his master returned abruptly, he punished him. Both men knew they had a charge to keep. They knew that the master would return and require a reckoning, but they didn't know the time of his arrival. The wise servant lived believing it; but the foolish servant said, "He delays his coming," and was shocked when his master came suddenly. So Christ says, "I am coming back. You don't know the hour, so get ready for it."

2. *The parable of the ten virgins* (Matt. 25:1-13). Jesus tells us the story of the five wise and the five foolish virgins. It was their duty to go forth to meet the bridegroom and escort him to the marriage chamber. But the bridegroom tarried and the virgins went to sleep. Then at midnight the cry was sounded, "Behold, the bridegroom cometh; go ye out to meet him." The five foolish virgins had no oil in their lamps, so they said to the wise ones, "Give us some of your oil." But the wise ones said, "We can't do that, for we have just enough for our own lamps. Go out and buy oil for yourselves." And while the foolish

virgins were gone, the bridegroom and the wise virgins went in to the marriage, and the door was shut.

Then the foolish virgins came back and sought to get in, but the sad answer came back, "I know you not." Here Jesus was referring to the time when He, the heavenly Bridegroom, would be coming back, for He ended the story by saying, "Watch therefore, for ye know neither the day nor the hour wherein the Son of man cometh."

Concerning the Lord's return, the Bible speaks of Jesus as the Bridegroom, as He is the bridegroom in this parable. The oil referred to is the symbol of the Holy Spirit. Those who have the oil are those who know Jesus Christ; those who have not the oil do not know Him. When He returns, some will be ready to meet Him, and some will not.

All the virgins had lamps and knew they were supposed to meet the bridegroom, yet some of them were admitted to the marriage feast and some were not. Isn't that telling us that all who profess religion do not know Christ? They go along with Christians, they look and act like them in some ways, but their profession is empty; they have never had a saving experience with the Lord. When the groom came, the foolish virgins discovered their lamps were empty. So they rushed about to get some oil, but they waited too late to prepare. So when Jesus comes in the air, I fear that many who have made empty professions will find they never really possessed Christ, but they'll find this out too late.

We note here also that when the bridegroom tarried the virgins went to sleep. They were aroused only when they heard the midnight cry. In the early Christian era men looked for Christ's coming. But while He tarried Satan lulled the church to sleep. She became busy with worldly things and earthly power. It has only been in the last half century that God has given us a revival of the truth of the blessed hope. His coming must be near.

A preacher told me that only since 1870 have men preached on the Second Coming, therefore he rejects it. But if we believe the New Testament we know Christ is coming back, even though this great truth has been sorely neglected. In the

Great Commission Jesus told believers to go into all the world with His message. For the first two centuries of the Christian era this was done, but then the commission was neglected for years. It has just been in the last hundred years that an interest in world-wide missions has been revived. Well, we can't reject the Second Coming any more than we can reject the Great Commission. The doctrine of our Lord's return is most important, even though it has often been neglected by preachers and Christian teachers.

As we think again of the parable of the ten virgins, we find that the message for our hearts is this: He is coming back, and He may come at any minute. Therefore let's be sure we have oil in our lamps. Let's be sure that we belong to Jesus and that we are ready to meet Him.

3. *Now notice Mark 13:33-37:* "Take ye heed, watch and pray: for ye know not when the time is. For the Son of man is as a man taking a far journey, who left his house, and gave authority to his servants, and to every man his work, and commanded the porter to watch. Watch ye therefore: for ye know not when the master of the house cometh, at even, or at midnight, or at the cockcrowing, or in the morning: lest coming suddenly he find you sleeping. And what I say unto you I say unto all, Watch." The teaching here is that our great Master has gone away but He will return. Since we don't know the exact hour, we should be watching and ready any minute.

4. *There is another warning in Luke 12:35-37:* "Let your loins be girded about, and your lights burning; and ye yourselves like unto men that wait for their lord, when he will return from the wedding; that when he cometh and knocketh, they may open unto him immediately. Blessed are those servants, whom the lord when he cometh shall find watching: verily I say unto you, that he shall gird himself, and make them sit down to meat, and will come forth and serve them." Jesus is telling Christians to be like these faithful servants, standing at the door, lamps lighted, peering into the darkness and listening eagerly for the steps of the Savior.

5. *Look at Luke 17:30,34-36:* "Even thus shall it be in the day when the Son of man is revealed. . . . I tell you, in that night

there shall be two men in one bed; the one shall be taken, and the other shall be left. Two women shall be grinding together; the one shall be taken, and the other left. Two men shall be in the field; the one shall be taken, and the other left." Here we see that Christ's coming will be unexpected and unannounced. It will occur while people are at their daily tasks, or while they are sleeping. He will come when He is least expected.

Here we see the scientific accuracy of the Bible. Just a few hundred years ago men learned that the world was round, that it could be night in one place while it is day in another. But the Bible told us this truth over 1,900 years ago when it said that He would come while some are working (that would be in the daytime), and while some were sleeping (that would be nighttime). So in all these passages Jesus speaks of the imminency of His coming and warns us to be ready at any moment.

II. THE APOSTLES SPOKE OF HIS IMMINENT COMING

1. *Romans 13:11,12* — "And that, knowing the time, that now it is high time to awake out of sleep: for now is our salvation nearer than when we believed. The night is far spent, the day is at hand: let us therefore cast off the works of darkness, and let us put on the armour of light." What salvation was Paul speaking of here? Not that of the soul, for Paul was already saved. He was speaking of the salvation of the body, which takes place when Jesus comes and takes our bodies up in the air.

In that day our salvation will be complete, and we'll be just like Him. We are incomplete and imperfect now. But we'll be complete and perfect then. "The night is far spent, the day is at hand." The present period is the period of darkness when Satan is active in the world. Jesus, the Light of the World, is now absent; but it will be glorious daybreak when He returns.

2. *Romans 16:20* — "And the God of peace shall bruise Satan under your feet shortly. The grace of our Lord Jesus Christ be with you. Amen." He hasn't bruised Satan yet as He will when He returns. The devil has a free rein now, but "shortly" Christ will crush his head, and he will never tempt us again.

3. *1 Corinthians 1:7* — "So that ye come behind in no gift;

waiting for the coming of our Lord Jesus Christ." Here Paul is telling the Corinthians not to get behind in anything. They must keep everything in good shape, knowing that Christ is coming back soon. We are to do the same. We are to keep up our spiritual work; we are to maintain good relationships with others; we are to keep all sin from coming between us and the Savior. The gift spoken of here could be the tithe we owe to God. We must keep that up so we'll not be behind when He comes.

4. *Hebrews 10:25* — "Not forsaking the assembling of ourselves together, as the manner of some is; but exhorting one another: and so much the more, as ye see the day approaching." We are being told here to be faithful in our church attendance, because the Lord may come at any moment and we want Him to find us faithful to His church.

5. *James 5:8* — "Be ye also patient; stablish your hearts: for the coming of the Lord draweth nigh." Here is another writer telling us that Christ's coming is imminent, that He may come at any moment.

III. THE BLESSINGS OF THE BLESSED HOPE

1. *The blessed hope is an incentive to right living.* We are told that if we have this hope we will purify ourselves. That's just natural. If we know Christ's coming is near and we must face Him to give account of our lives, we will try to live so as not to be ashamed when we meet Him.

All believers are one body in Christ, so the truth of His return was for the whole body of all ages. If He had told His people that He would return in the twentieth century, the people of the first century would have felt it didn't apply to them. They might not have lived for Him as they should have. So He didn't give us the exact date of His coming, which means that Christians of all ages are exhorted to live in the light of His soon return.

2. *The blessed hope brings comfort.* In talking to the Thessalonians, Paul said, "Don't be concerned that your loved ones who have died will miss anything. Jesus is coming, and then we'll all be together with Him; so comfort your hearts with this

thought." If they had known it would be two thousand years before He came back, there would have been little comfort in this for them. Jesus wanted this hope to live in every generation to bring comfort to every sorrowing heart.

3. *The blessed hope produces patience.* James told the Christians of his day to be "patient unto the coming of the Lord." These people were poor and were being ground to pieces by wicked and wealthy employers. They wondered if their suffering would ever end. James told them to be patient. The Lord would relieve and reward them at His coming. Today many Christians are bearing burdens. Often it seems that there is no relief in sight. The only hope they have is in the coming of Christ. They can be more patient as they remember that deliverance is nigh.

4. *The blessed hope is an antidote to worry.* In Philippians 4:5,6, Paul says, "The Lord is at hand. Be careful for nothing." He is telling us not to worry because one day the Lord will return and straighten everything out. We worry about conditions national, international, and personal. We have problems of health, high taxes, and high prices — and many other problems. But why should Christians worry when they can trust? We may soon go to be with Christ in paradise, or He may come back any day to take us home.

Jesus made the blessed hope a practical thing. He withheld the time of His coming so that this truth would apply to men of every century. All along we are to remember that His coming is imminent. Each morning as we awake we can say, "Perhaps today, Lord," and be strengthened by this hope as we set about the tasks of the day.

IV. WHY DOES OUR LORD TARRY?

Why has the era of millennial blessing been postponed? Why does He allow a sinful world to go on? Why does He not return and take His blood-washed children to glory? No one can give you a complete answer to these questions. "Now we see through a glass darkly." But let us try to give a partial answer to the question as to why His coming is delayed, yet always imminent.

1. *Maybe He tarries so that men will finally recognize the world's need of a perfect leader.* God has given man every opportunity to rule and regenerate the world. And man has gone forth in his conceit and said, "Yes, I can do it, just watch my smoke." What has been the result? Nothing but smoke. Every scheme of man to make a perfect world has failed.

Man talks of improvement, education, advancement, enlightenment, and civilization as he boasts of his greatness. Still the courts are filled with criminals; wars continue to ravish nations; inhumanities abound; and homes, hearts, and hopes are blasted by sin. Man can't make a better world because he is too sinful himself. Maybe Christ is waiting until the whole world recognizes this failure and feels more keenly the need, not of a Superman, but of a Supernatural Man. Then, when the harvest is ripe, He whose place it is to reign forever will come.

2. *Maybe He tarries to display His long-sufferance.* For nearly two thousand years Christ has been saying, "Come unto Me." He has been dealing with the world in mercy and not in judgment. We often say, "Look at the conditions in the world today. Look at what men are doing. Why doesn't God put a stop to it?" It is because He is patient and long-suffering. Some of you may be forty or fifty years of age, yet you are still lost; you are outside of Christ. Suppose He had come ten or twenty years ago? You would have perished in your sin. Let us thank God for His long-sufferance and let us be grateful that He has tarried long enough to give you a chance to be saved.

3. *Maybe He tarries to fully test the faith of His children.* This has always been God's way. Why did Abraham have to wait so long to receive Isaac? Why did God allow Israel to remain so long in bondage in Egypt? Why did four thousand years elapse between the promise of His coming and His actual entrance into the world? Maybe it was all because God was testing His people, wanting them to demonstrate the reality of their confidence in Him.

Why has Jesus tarried so long in the Father's house? Why has the church journeyed for all these years in the wilderness? Though millions today look up for His coming, why are the heavens still silent? Maybe it is because God is testing His people. Maybe He wants to show the angels He has a people He can trust, even amid the darkness and sin of this present generation.

Scoffers still cry, "Where is the promise of His coming? Things are as they have always been." Yet He will come even as He promised. Then we'll understand everything. We'll know that there was a good purpose in His delay and that God does all things well.

So here is where we stand right now. Christ is coming. The date is not known, but He may come at any minute. Therefore both Christians and the unsaved ought to get ready to meet Him. In the closing scene in the Bible, when John is on the Isle of Patmos, the Savior speaks to him, saying, "Surely I come quickly." And the aged apostle and lover of his Lord replies, "Even so, come, Lord Jesus." Oh, that his prayer would be answered today! I want Him to come, don't you?

In Arizona there is a peculiar grave. Behind it is a tragic yet wonderful story. Many years ago a tribe of Indians came together for a "pow-wow." They felt they were sinners and needed to do something about it. Somehow they felt that blood must be shed for an atonement. The chief said that it had to be human blood. So they decided a child should be sacrificed, since he had less sin than the others.

The chief then went from one warrior to another and asked the question, "Will you give your child?" Each one answered, "No." When the chief was asked if he would give his child, he also answered, "No." Finally one of them said, "There are four orphans in our tribe. We can offer them." This was agreed upon. A large grave was dug, the four orphans were slain and buried in that grave. The poor Indians felt their sins had been atoned for. They didn't know of the precious blood of God's Lamb shed on Calvary's cross.

Yes, there was a time when we were guilty of sin. We needed atonement and salvation that comes only through the shedding of blood. So our great, loving heavenly Father said, "I'll give my Boy; I'll let my Son shed His blood for all mankind." And Christ did just that on a dark day just outside the city wall on a hill called Golgotha.

Isn't it wonderful! The blood has been shed; our salvation is a finished work. We can come to Him now and have our sins washed away; then we'll be ready to meet Him when He comes. Hallelujah! Amen!